MW00464404

*All-Beneficent Ra-Hoor-Khuit*
by Kat Lunoe
*see explanation page x*

# Tantric Thelema

*&*

*The Invocation of Ra-Hoor-Khuit*
*in the manner of*
*the Buddhist Mahayoga Tantras*

Sam Webster, M.Div., Mage

Concrescent Press

Copyright 2010 by J.A. Sam Webster Mayers

All rights reserved. Except for brief quotations in a review, the book, or parts thereof, including the cover art and interior illustrations, must not be reproduced in any work without permission in writing from the publisher. For information contact Concrescent Press, Richmond CA, USA

www.Concrescent.net
info@concrescent.net

ISBN: 978-0-9843729-0-4

Library of Congress Control Number:  2010900063

Revision 1.2

Section XII "The Three Refuges" from The Collected Works of Aleister Crowley, Volume II, (© Ordo Templi Orientis, 1906, 2009), the first verse of Liber Cordis Cincti Serpente vel ADNI (© Ordo Templi Orientis, 1909, 2009) and quotes from the Book of the Law used with permission.

It is said by Lochen Dharamsari,

In Mahayoga one realizes all phenomena
as the magical display of ultimate mind,
the indivisibility of appearance and emptiness.

In Anuyoga, one realizes all phenomena
as manifestive power of the ultimate mind,
the indivisibility of the ultimate sphere and wisdom.

In Atiyoga, one realizes that all phenomena
are self appearances of the ultimate mind,
the spontaneously arisen wisdom,
which is primordially free from arising and cessation.

## Acknowledgments

My thanks go to the early readers of this book: Barbara Cormack, Anodea Judith, and Denny Sargent. Your insight and advice was invaluable. To Kat Lunoe who produced the gorgeous cover art. To Lena Strayhorn for her sharp proofing eye. Any errors remaining, of fact or form, are mine. Finally, to Amy Hale, my last reader, who gave me the confidence that this book really did make sense.

I also wish to gratefully acknowledge the many dozens of practitioners who have learned the rituals in this book from me, especially the early ones who had to tolerate my learning how to teach them, particularly Michael Sanborn, who experimented with it in new contexts, and the members of the Open Source Order of the Golden Dawn who regularly use them. I learned as much from them as they from me.

*This work is dedicated*
*to my Wife*

**Mary Margaret Tara Ashilanah Whittaker Webster-Mayers**
**January 8, 1963 to October 8, 2008**

*In Memoriam*

# Confession

*I am not a Lama. I am nobody's Guru.*

The work herein is composed on the basis of my best knowledge and most was practiced for many years before teaching. I think it worthwhile but your mileage may vary.

I don't teach Buddhism, but I do see this work as a implementation of the Buddhadharma. If you want to learn Vajrayana, go find a competent teacher and do the work. I have nothing but the greatest respect for the Lamas and nothing in this book should be construed otherwise.

What is offered here is an enhancement of Thelema and a support for the practice of Magick.

Magick without Bodhicitta is Death.

Magick devoted to the benefit of all beings makes the world whole.

We need to get better at this, and that is the purpose of this body of work.

If there is any harm herein,
may it fall upon me.
If there is any good herein,
may its benefit be dedicated to
the complete liberation and supreme enlightenment
of all beings, everywhere, pervading space and time.

*Sam Webster*

# The All-Beneficent Ra-Hoor-Khuit

*I ask you to sacrifice nothing at mine altar;*
*I am the God who giveth all.*
Liber Tzaddi v20

The cover art is a specific form of the principal godform of this body of practice. It was developed through dialogue and inspiration with the artist, Kat Lunoe, who executed the original in oils.

*Ra-Hoor-Khuit has the head of a hawk and a human body with blue-black skin. His head shows His consummate perspicacity and His skin shows His source in the Ground of Being. He is crowned with the solar disk in which arises the emerald Uraeus. The disk shows His compassionate, provident, and wrathful power and the Uraeus, His relentless drive. His human body shows He has taken up the Middle Way, free from the extremes of monism, dualism, eternalism or nihilism. He wears the collar of seven metals and twelve gems for the planets and the Zodiac and shows that His horizon is the Universe. He wears a white kilt belted with gold, gold ornaments, and His nemmes is sky blue barred with gold. The kilt shows His innate purity, the gold belt and ornaments, the fullness of His capabilities, and the nemmes, that His view is as wide as the sky. He is seated on a 49-petaled red rose entwined with white jasmine, showing the female and male potentials that give rise to His being. He is in the lotus posture to show His absolute stability. In His right hand is the wast, the double scepter, while His left is empty. The scepter is His rulership of form while His empty hand shows His rulership of the formless. He is winged to show His beneficent protection and all-pervading generosity. He is surrounded by flames to show His limitless energy. He is seated between the papyrus and lily of the Two Lands of Egypt to show His dominion over the whole world. Over His head are Hadit and Nuit, of Whose union He is a manifestation.*

*Before Him are His working tools: a dorje, a phurba, a chopper, a skull-bowl and hand-bell. His wast is pinning a serpent representing all obstacles, looking up at Him in gratitude for its liberation.*

*Offerings are placed before Him. A bowl of twelve gems to represent the Zodiac, six bars of metal to represent six of the seven planets, eight bowls to represent the four elements, ether and the three alchemical principles. With the sistrum, an offering of music and the mirror, representing both the planet Mercury and mind, all of the senses are likewise offered. The roses are there because He likes them. The two Trees of Life, aright and averse, complete the offering to Him of the entire Cosmos.*

*This particular form of Ra-Hoor-Khuit, called the All-Beneficent, is specifically an embodiment of His enriching and increasing powers.*

# Contents

# List of Practices

# Preface

Postmodern critical theory teaches us that all texts are read through a frame or world view which highly conditions the interpretation of the text. Texts that admit of interpretations from multiple points of view, or frames, demonstrate therein their own richness, depth, and sometimes sanctity.

Liber AL vel Legis, also called the Book of the Law, or Liber AL (AL) as well as the other Crowleyan and non-Crowleyan Thelemic Holy Books evince these properties. There are roughly tens of thousands of Thelemites the world over, and of those I've met across the U.S., as well as the significant number of international visitors, their views of Thelema and its texts are at least as numerous as the number of persons. There are clusters of opinion, but we can hardly expect anything other than a rich ecology of ideas from this highly individualistic tradition.

Another important factor in the interpretation or understanding of a text is knowing its genera, especially with texts of spiritual import. Galileo fell afoul of this when the verse from Psalm 19v6 saying the sun moved, "its going forth is from the end of the heavens, his circuit to its ends," was taken as a scientific statement by the Catholic Church, and not as poetry.

In Western terms Liber AL is clearly some kind of apocalypse, as it makes a claim of revelation. However, it also has many elements congruent with the Indian genre of text called 'Tantra', which are sacred to the tradition of the same name. In particular, the Buddhist Tantras tend to have the characteristics of presenting a theory and goal of practice, a means or vehicle of practice and a divine form that embodies the practice and its successful outcome.

For the purpose of this work we will adopt the view of the Book of the Law as a Tantra, all the while knowing many other 'readings' co-exist. From this viewpoint will be drawn a body of practice to enable the user to attain to the realization Thelema promises.

What that realization is, each must determine for themselves. For me, it is a non-climaxing process whereby I integrate my actions with the All [cosmos, god] through contemplating the conundrum that my will is a manifestation of and inalienably united with the Divine Will of the Totality of Being, achieving harmony with the world while in life, and freedom in death. With the tools of Theurgy and Tantra, the Thelemic Mage advances upon the path.

This work builds on the Pagan Dharma articles published in *Gnosis* and *Pangaia* magazines in the 1990s and kept on-line at www.OSOGD.org. They give an introduction to my view and some preliminary practices. Both have been updated and included herein. What those articles did not cover are the forms of Deity Yoga of which those preliminary techniques are parts. What follows is a method of Deity Yoga used in the Vajrayana composed in a manner useful to Pagan magick-users. It also assumes significant knowledge and skill in magick. It is not a beginner text, but an intermediate or advanced one.

All of the methods below have been 'beta-tested' through my own psyche and have proven efficacious, although some of the later practices in this book not as much as the earlier. Since I am not a Lama, nevermind a Buddha, I cannot guarantee that this is a correct interpretation of the Tibetan methodology, but I believe this will be of help to us all.

So as to not encroach on Tibetan Buddhism's proprietary domain, and although their methods are long published, a design constraint was accepted to apply the formulae of invocation without using their words and letters. This would be a theft of identity and culture and thus unjustifiable. But using the principles as published and duly translated is righteous as a recovery or a replacement of our own lost technology. Further, it is justified because we need the medicine these practices provide. Also, no Lamas' names have been mentioned as they have no responsibility for this work.

For the sake of exposition, the ancient and traditional mode of dialogue is adopted. Early in writing this work it became an epistle written to my wife and magickal partner of eighteen years. She at times offered her own viewpoint on the teachings, illuminating them. I am forever in her debt for improving my writing down these years and for listening while this work was being crafted. This way is rooted in relationship. It is hoped that relationship will illuminate its character.

*Ancora Imparo*
[I am still learning]
Before the Western Gate of the World at San Francisco Bay
Autumn 2009

# 1

# Entering the Buddhadharma

*Thus I have made up...*

Beloved, you have accompanied me on this long journey to find the depth and meaning of Thelema, the Dharma and Tantra, experiencing the travails, failures and successes of this path with me. So, it is mete and proper, since I have been asked to write this small book, to write it to you. I know no one more receptive or properly curious about this subject so I will attempt to put in text the ways and means whereby you, I, and all others who walk this way may be able to read the Thelemic Holy Books as Tantras.

This is mostly a manual of practice, but as *Praxis* can not stand without *Theoria*, I will lightly explain the hows and whys. Certainly when it comes to the Dharma and Tantra, there are older, wiser and better informed sources than I. I would counsel their study as that will deepen and enrich your practice. Thelema is a more difficult issue in that much has been written but in that writing is much confusion. However, this text as a whole can be seen as an interpretation of the Thelemic Holy Books in general and the Book of the Law, Liber AL, in particular. I hope this will be sufficient and helpful.

I have written snippets about this subject in various fora so I will include some of that herein. Mostly, after some preliminary explanations to set our symbols and harmonize our conceptions, this text will explore practices that demonstrate the principles of Thelema and Tantra directly, since these paths lie beyond reason in the stubborn and irreducible empyric.

Dear One, let us start with Thelema it is as the less public and lesser known side of our path. At base, Thelema is a body of practice and thought rooted in a text of two hundred and twenty verses written in 1904 by Aleister Crowley called the Book of the Law. A number of years later under inspiration he wrote a set of companion texts that further illuminate this path. Over the many years since a number of individuals upon reaching a certain phase in their practice have also written inspired texts rooted in the same source and with similar symbolism. Depending on the predilections of the reader these latter texts may or may not be considered along with Crowley's writings as part of the body of literature called collectively the Holy Books of Thelema.

Like many spiritual paths, Thelema concentrates on a single focus as the vehicle or impetus along the way. 'Thelema,' the word itself, is Greek meaning 'will.' Thelema is thus a path that engages primarily with the core ethical question, "What am I to do?" Thelema posits an 'answer' that is not an answer but a focus for attention and practice: "Do your will." This 'will' is seen as the innate presence of the Absolute Divine incarnate within every individual entity. The practice is to continually center our behavior upon this divine presence and let that be the guide to our actions. This strips away the lists of rules and regulations and demands of us the highest integrity in all we do. I know of no other ethical system that reaches this lofty plane. No thelemite, as we are called, can ever say that we did some evil because the rules said we could or should. The responsibility for our actions rests squarely on our own shoulders, and nowhere else.

This practice is especially difficult in the beginning. The neophyte must pass though many ordeals in coming to know what his or her will is and what are the right actions to be derived of it. Many have read the Book of the Law with mammalian eyes and seen in it an excuse to abuse those around them. These, the text itself warns, have fallen into the pit called Because and surely shall perish with the dogs of Reason for preying upon their neighbors. But more importantly, what value would there be in a text that tells us to return to a dog-eat-dog world? No! Only the foolish would read the text thus and they deserve the consequences.

But one who perseveres through the ordeals of this knowledge comes to a deep understanding of their integrity with the Living World and takes up their own part in ever-unfolding Cosmogenesis. It is for these, like yourself, My Love, that this book is writ. These participate in the great Law that is Love, knowing that Relationship is ordained and inextricable. In that fundamental unity, they find the right way of doing that relationship by manifesting forth the divinely given desire that is our individual will. Thus Love is the Law, Love under Will.

To this high and holy end we are given in the sundry texts methods and means whereby we can attain to and pass through the ordeals that lead unto this knowledge and thus eventually to the fullest articulation and accomplishment of our wills. After one hundred years the range of known practice is vast. We will take up the Tantric view in approaching this text as it illuminates many valuable elements.

We have no choice in the interpretation of our core text. Even though some claim that this is forbidden or that the discussion of our interpretations are forbidden, without discussion how can others benefit from our experience, our successes or our failures? No, this view is both false and hypocritical since it is *itself* an interpretation, and a restrictive one. If those who hold to this view would come out of their cave into the light of thousands of years of scriptural study they would know where that art stands today: every reader reads the text uniquely, none can tell another what the text would mean to that other, but each in sharing what they have seen enriches the other. This present writing is an offering to that end, that others may benefit from what I have seen and go yet farther.

Dearest, we also need to speak somewhat of Tantra. This Sanskrit word derived of 'to weave,' refers to the continuum of being and of mind. It arises when liturgical and magickal practices are placed in the service of attaining to enlightenment. While arising in India, it is close kin if not of the same flesh as the Classical Western practice of Theurgy and so easily understood by Western magickal users. Tech is Tech, and the tantrikas use the same tech we do but with the overlay of Indo-Tibetan culture. The particular variety that I work with is the Buddhist form of Tantra, which is both cosmopolitan (open to outsiders) and exquisitely focused on the attainment of enlightenment now.

One of my teachers taught that Vajrayana, one name for Tantric Buddhism, is not culturally bound. One of the goals of this work is to begin formulating a Western Tantric tradition. I have talked a bit about this on-line in the past so I will include here what I called "Entering the Buddhadharma" on the Chthonic Ouranian Order's listserv, August 2002.

*I find when exploring a new current the guardians of the current tend to take an interest in me until I resolve my relationship to that current. This is rarely a comfortable thing.*

*So, my exploration of things 'Buddhist' has not been easy or gentle, but it has been very fruitful. It began simply by taking a class in seminary on "Tibetan Contemplative Tradition" along with other classes on various other religions as a way of broadening my knowledge.*

*It was in this class that I met a Lama and was given the explanation of refuge, "We all need help, Refuge is asking for help." For a variety of reasons this really worked for me. While important, this understanding of refuge was not the most impactful thing I got from him at the time. It was a practice called "Benefit for Beings Pervading Space" and the reason was because I could do it. This practice invokes Chenrezig, a.k.a. Avalokiteshvara, the Boddhisattva of Compassion and wields that compassion through the mantra "Om Mani Peme Hung" to remediate the suffering of the six classes of beings caught in samsara.*

*Samsara, sometimes translated as "cyclical existence," is called 'Kor-wa' in Tibetan, meaning "running in circles." The idea is that these are beings who have no control as to how they incarnate or the condition of their lives. They are entirely enmeshed in their karma and this is unsatisfactory to them. The six classes of beings benefited by this practice are Gods, Jealous Gods (called by the Greeks 'Titans'), Humans, Animals, Hungry Ghosts and Hell Beings.*

There is a lot in here that I have to gloss over but suffice it to say that the purpose of the rite is to remove some of the suffering of each of these kinds of beings in turn through the power of the mantra. Where this gets interesting is that while driving home from practice I kept finding myself filled with anger and other unpleasant emotions. And I could not get them to stop.

They became overwhelming. I was curled up in bed screaming, overloaded with all kinds of anguish and could not get my grounding. Through roundabout means I got a question to the Lama describing my condition and asking for advice. His reply was that I should rejoice.

Apparently it usually takes years of practice before one learns how to tie into the ground of suffering. I had done so in just a few sessions. The ground of suffering is the space or energy of the suffering of all beings. Those who can wield compassion to drain that domain and transform it into pleasure or power or wisdom, or whatever.

I was tying into the ground of suffering but I was not performing the transformation because I did not realize that the mantra was the tool with which to do the transform. Once this was explained to me, I knew exactly what to do. I wielded the mantra, fed it the suffering I was being overwhelmed with, and instantly the feelings were transformed into intense pleasure and energy.

None of this was because I am in any way special. It is because I am a mage and I can work magick, like any of you.

So, I continued to study. The next big piece for me was Steven Beyer's The Cult of Tara. This work is a highly detailed study of a set of Tibetan rituals. Interestingly to me, in order to explain Tibetan ritual magick, Beyer had to turn to the Western tradition, in fact to all of those names we know and love: Ficino, Agrippa, Levi, Crowley, etc.. This work is for me a Rosetta stone, one that showed me that the techniques of so-called 'oriental' ritual magick are no different than those of the Western tradition. It is just that their culture dedicated the same energy to ritual the West dedicated to music, so when it comes to ritual, while we are playing three chord rock & roll, they are playing symphonies.

But, tech is tech. The same principals used there are used here. In fact I found in this book the very method described in the Asclepius, the brief description in the Hermetic Corpus of drawing the daemon of a star into a statue to animate it. In The Cult of Tara, the statue was one of Tara, but here the full method and its theory were spelled out. I can attest to the fact that it works.

Now to Thelema. Uncle Al [as we fondly refer to Aleister Crowley], considered the Book of the Law as a sort of third testament. Appealing as that is, as a student of Western religion I've studied the genres of the scriptures and it doesn't quite fit. The closest thing to it is an apocalypse since it reveals something, but those usually involve someone being taken up to heaven or having a vision revealed in the temple. This one is different.

However there is a genre that very nicely matches Liber AL. In this genre a cosmology is often expressed, a specific view to practice is given and a godform is presented for the practitioner to wear. This genre is the kind of text called a tantra.

When I got exposed to the Buddhadharma I began to see Thelema in the stream of those working for the greater evolutionary purpose. It, and the rest of the Western *stream, the Hermetic, Rosicrucian, Alchymical, and others, I saw as part of one large process going on on this world, transcendent to any particular culture. (There have also been hints of this going on on other worlds). As I discovered the unity of Western and Eastern tech and so began to press on my understanding of the split, I came to realize that there was none save a historical division caused by the rise of Christianity and Islam.*

*In the Nyingma tradition of Tibetan Buddhism there is a peculiar version of continuous revelation. Texts, called 'termas' or treasures, would be delivered to individuals who would be given the task of writing them down or figuring out how to apply them.*

*Pick your mythology as you will, in essence all such texts come from the fundamental Ground of Being out of which we all arise which is compassionate, intelligent and provident. The evidence for this is the Cosmos itself. In its continual process of trying to help us, it creates things like tantric texts. I think Liber AL is one of these.*

*Crowley had a hard time accepting "existence is pure joy" being a rationalist Buddhist at the time, but that was mostly due to a lack of education. From the fact that in the Thoth Deck, one of the last products of his life, we see in the Two of Wands and the Ten of Wands that he does not know the difference between a dorje and a phurba we can tell he never made contact with the Tantric or Vajrayana stream of Buddhism. This is the magick-using part of Buddhism. This is also the part of Buddhism that would very well understand what is going on the in the Book of the Law, if they could only get through the code and Golden Dawn symbolism.*

*I'm not going to do a complete analysis here but for instance many people have trouble with the presentation of the Ra-Hoor-Khuit in the third chapter. However anyone who has read the practice of a wrathful Buddha would consider Ra-Hoor-Khuit only mildly wrathful. Stamping down on the wretched and the weak is a gentle approach to correcting suffering compared to some of the actions of the dakinis.*

*However, this I will point out: Thelema is the first current in the West that roots itself in the Not. This is what the Buddhists call 'shunyata,' poorly translated as 'the void.' H.V. Guenther, the Tibetologist, translates the term as "the sphere whose center is everywhere and its circumference is nowhere." Also, the 'Dharma', translated 'Law', is based on the awareness of this shunyata and is its fundamental key, i.e., 61, 8, 80, 418, if you take my meaning.*

*So these are the parallels I make: Nuit is Prajñaparamita, the perfection of wisdom embodied, shunyata given a face and form, the mother of all the Buddhas (Buddha means awakened one), and the basis for all refuge. Hadit is the inherent buddha-nature within each of us, already enlightened or 'perfect.' Ra-Hoor-Khuit is the union of entitative being (Hadit) and world (Nuit) and is the godform or Yi-dam for Thelemites to take in their practice as a way of articulating their will. (Not necessarily all the time but as an archetype).*

*I've shared with you a refuge verse I composed on the spot previously:*

In the ground of being, from which all things arise,
In the inherently enlightened nature within each and everyone,
In the inexorable causation the magi know,
I take refuge.

*If I were to spin this back around to Thelemic terminology it would be:*
Nu is my refuge
as Hadit my light
and Ra-Hoor-Khu
is the strength, force,
vigor of my arms.

*For me the proof of the pudding is in the tasting. I used the methodology mentioned above and many of its components to build a set of rituals using the Thelemic godforms and symbolism and used the View, the insight gained from the Buddhadharma to focus it. In one of these Ra-Hoor-Khuit is the deity-form the practitioner takes on in exactly the same 'Buddhist' manner. Yet the ritual is entirely Thelemic.*

*For me there is that which lies beyond all of our cultural view points that drives all sentient beings towards their complete happiness. The Buddhadharma and Thelema are two manifestations of this same source and as such have harmonious union.*

*I eventually took refuge with a Lama to make peace with the guardians of the Buddhadharma, to further commit myself to the great work of bringing happiness to all beings, and to unite within myself two approaches to the same goal.*

*For me, I have one life, thus one path, and I find value in uniting in that path the truth however and wherever I find it."*

My Dearest, for the amusement of those so concerned, if I were challenged by someone about the origins of Liber AL or its author and the possibility of reading it as a tantra, in a playful mood I would say that Aiwaz is one of the secret names of Padmasambhava.

*Om Ah Hung Vajra Guru Pame Aiwaz Hung!*

After all, who can say that it is not?

Having laid out the elements of what we have to work with, let's get to the work.

## Table of Relationships

| Thelema | Buddha-Dharma | Translation & Referent |
|---|---|---|
| Nuit | Prajñaparamita or Shunyata | Void or Nun |
| Hadit | Tathagatagharba | Buddha-Nature |
| Ra-Hoor-Khuit | Yi-dam | Mind-Protector & Godform |

# 2

# Taking Refuge, Dedicating Merit

My Love, we have a long road ahead of us to explore Tantric Thelema. Both knowledge and skill must be acquired before we can approach understanding. Since this work is focused on practice we'll let practice drive the explanation.

*Husband, before we go so deep, give me again the Pagan Dharma teachings. I want them refreshed in my mind before we go on...*

As you will, My Love. They begin with a call for help. . .

*Hail to the Tathagatagharba in all beings!*

Our era of profound spiritual crisis is equally an era of spiritual foment rivaled only by that time two thousand years ago that saw the emergence of Gnosticism, Christianity, and the Hermetic Tradition in the West and Mahayana Buddhism and Vedanta in the East. Today, as then, this transformative crisis is being fueled by the confluence of cultures, none of which will remain the same for that contact. Two such cultures, contemporary Paganism and Tibetan or Vajrayana Buddhism, have the potential to deeply revitalize each other and positively effect our world.

Paganism has survived awful abuse for seventeen hundred years. It is a testimony to the vitality and resilience of the culture that it survives in any form today. Outside of the Catholic and Orthodox Churches, possibly Masonry and perhaps the Jews, contemporary Paganism preserves the only remaining living ritual tradition in the West. Protestantism has vestiges of ritual in baptism and such rites but mostly is a preaching tradition. Even the High

Churches have preserved only a narrow range of ritual practice. The Pagans however still create rituals from generative grammars as needed to supplement the more established forms. Yet due to the abuse the tradition has experienced the degree of self-critical reflection and refinement of that ritual tradition is very thin. At most we have only a generation or two's examination of our process, which, while helpful, is no match for a thousand years of sustained attention.

Over the years of practicing Pagan magickal ritual I have noticed a variety of consistent problems with our practice. Many solutions for these have been attempted with varying success. When I was introduced to the Tibetan contemplative tradition (read Vajrayana), one of the points my teacher made was how the practitioners noted problems with their practices and with insight (and I suspect lots of trial and error and sharing results) they were able to solve them. Indeed, he noted, most books of Tibetan ritual practice were structured with the first chapter or so giving the practice itself and the remaining many chapters delineating all the ways the practice could go wrong and how to fix them. He also shared some of the more general techniques and what they were remedies for. Perhaps because ritual is ritual and it is humans doing it regardless of where on the world they are, the same problems he mentioned among the Buddhists I had seen among Pagans. Shamelessly, and in true Hermetic manner, I began applying some of the remedies in my own ritual practice and with my community. Needless to say they helped.

One of these that was very easy to adopt was the dedication of the benefit of the ritual to all beings (this of course includes the ritual practitioners). Either by verbally dedicating the benefit in this manner or by 'sweeping' the good that we have done into an energy ball in the center of the ritual space and tossing it up into the sky to rain down on all beings, we were easily able to incorporate this ritual element. However effective as this sharing might be, the most immediate benefit to the group was the complete absence of the post-ritual blues, ungroundedness and general irritability that I and many other practitioners have experienced. Instead a calm sense of satisfaction tends to pervades the space.

Another more pervasive issue among magickal practitioners is the problem of magick going awry or causing harm, which it can easily do since it is refracted through our subconscious (thus not wholly under our conscious control) and since it is simply a power of nature. With our practice of magick comes an interaction with the world that requires, due to its power, a deeper level of responsibility and accountability in life than for non-practitioners. Instead, we regularly cause trouble for ourselves, but this is more due to a lack of skill than necessity.

Looking back over our history, I wonder if, in the frightful need to transmit the *how*, the Western Magical Tradition lost the *why*. In the face of oppression and ridicule the practice of magick was nearly, but not successfully, exterminated. But those who transmitted the core of our way forward in time did not include as inherent the process of rooting our work in compassion.

Its absence today, this lack of high intention, cripples us. Though we value the Earth and root to it when we do our work, this is not enough to place the momentum of the greatest good for all behind our magickal efforts, our spells and rites. Yet by generating compassion we can invoke the inherent power of the entire Universe driving us all toward our eventual enlightenment to strengthen and fulfill our magick.

The Buddhists call this 'Bodhicitta' and make a particular point of generating it at the beginning of every ritual. This is also what the Mahayana Buddhadharma brought to the magick users of India and Tibet, giving rise to Buddhist Tantra and the Vajrayana. This names means Diamond or Lightning Vehicle, and is the ritual magic using part of Buddhism.

Vajrayana is what happens when a magickal culture becomes Buddhist and decides on Compassion. And is not compassion needed by every person, organization, business, government, etc.? Thus a practice that makes a virtue of compassion/Bodhicitta would be helpful to and for all. But, when done by magick users it is particularly powerful. Is it not our responsibility, since we have the power, to invoke compassionate action? In a deep sense this is a means of casting a vote in the ultimate franchise by determining what kind of world we live in.

The great hope that we can integrate Vajrayana practice in Pagan ritual is made clear by Stephen Beyer's work *The Cult of Tara*. There he shows that the only way to interpret Tibetan ritual practice is to take seriously their view of the reality of magick. To do this Beyer had to turn to the Western magickal tradition to find useful categories of analysis. When he returned with these tools to the Tibetan culture, he found that the same (not merely similar) methods were being used in both traditions. I note in my study that the principal difference, besides the presence of the Buddhist view, is that the Tibetan techniques are much more thorough.

The structural identity of the two systems permits us to conclude that should the Pagani adopt the practice of generating Bodhicitta they will (potentially) achieve the same result, a compassion-based practice that is both effective and helpful to self and others.

The contemporary Pagan and Magickal communities share an oddly interconnected history with the Buddhadharma. While some scholars have suggested connections between classical Paganism and the classical Far East ,and some connections may be found during the Renaissance, it is with the first translations of the Eastern holy texts into European languages that the initial and most obvious effect appears and that in reaction. Christopher McIntosh, in his biography of Eliphas Levi, determined that one of Levi's motivations was a sense that it is all well and good that the Eastern traditions have all these esoteric spiritual practices, but so has the West—we just have to dig harder. And so while the Transcendentalists and German Romantics were enraptured by the Upanishads, the Bhagavad-Gita, and the Pali Canon, Levi was fusing Hebraic Kabbalah with the Tarot and goetic conjurations and Paracelsian elemental work with Agrippa's redaction of classical theurgy.

Within a generation Madame Blavatsky would be in contact with "the Tibetan" and other teachers from the orient and claimed that her Secret Doctrine was rooted in Buddhist teachings. While this last was debatable due to the doctrine of the soul she presented being contrary to fundamental Buddhist teachings, both the text and her teachings show evidence of Buddhist philosophy intertwined with Western 'occult' thought. Joscelyn Godwin tracks this process in his *Theosophical Enlightenment*.

In the next generation, Aleister Crowley takes up the same attraction to Buddhism in its Sri Lankan form partly under the tutelage of Alan Bennett, his principal teacher of magick. Crowley later integrated the yogic techniques they learned from their mutual native teacher with magickal practice, and further blended some Buddhist principles into the Thelemic Holy Books, notably Liber B vel Magus. Bennett went even farther by abandoning magick and becoming a Buddhist monk, the second Westerner to do so. He formed the Buddhist Society of Great Britain and Ireland, an organization to bring Buddhism to the West, but the severe monastic tradition he brought was not readily accepted by Europeans. Godwin, at the end of his book, wonders what it would have been like if Bennett and Crowley had discovered Tantric Buddhism, the Vajrayana or Tibetan Buddhism. What would have happened then?

One of the key features of Buddhism is its thrust towards enlightenment. The classical Pagan tradition had similar goals. Plato had his aspiration towards Beauty through philosophy, Plotinus towards the One through contemplation. The Mystery traditions were said to free the aspirant from the fear of death and secure a pleasant afterlife. Christianity itself holds out the hope of heaven. Yet, while in each of these systems the ultimate aim was clearly formulated, in contemporary Paganism the goal is vague. Some speak of enlightenment, or of attaining unity with the Godhead (Goddess-head?) or perhaps some particular deity. Ceremonialists have inherited the Renaissance goal of the divinization of the Mage, Prospero's attainment of becoming one with the Cosmos and being able to wield its power. However, the methods of attainment are unclear.

Even this being the case, I would still contend that the strongest notions about our goal in Pagan practice are deeply influenced by the impact of Eastern religions on our society. Any ideas we have about enlightenment are qualified by our apprehension of Buddhist concepts of Nirvana and the Vedanta Hindu Moksha or Liberation. Some of this comes from the historical intertwining of Buddhism with the Magical tradition. Some of this comes from the efflorescence of the Sixties, formative years for the current Pagan revival, and some far older, such as the Jain influence in pre-Alexandrian times.

Nonetheless there is a certain alien quality to these views with respect to the contemporary Pagan view of the divineness of the Earth. Each of them postulates that there is some place else, some place better, where we would rather be. This is Gnostic dualism, and leads, as amply demonstrated by our current ecological crisis, to the denigration of the here and now, of the world on which we live, even of our bodies and the pleasure available in the immediate moment.

But when we push past the initial understandings of Buddhism, past the Theravada/Hinayana, past the Mahayana, we can find in the most exalted forms of Buddhism a view that corresponds directly to the Pagan view of the sanctity of the immediate. It is in the Vajrayana of Tantric Buddhism and in Dzog-Chen, "the Great Perfection" that we find an explicit positive valuation of the world and the body.

In Vajrayana, the challenging aspects of the world are not avoided, like the Theravadin, or antidoted as in Mahayana, but embraced and transformed into pristine and purified 'wisdoms.' The Vajrayana practitioner strives to experience all sound as mantra (divine speech), all vision as mandala (divine image) as well as all the senses pure and holy, and all beings as Goddesses and Gods, something H.V. Guenther calls the "symbolic recreation of the world."

In a sense, Pagans strive to do no less. One less than ultimate goal of Paganism is to live in a world that is loved and respected and cared for by all the people in it. To do this most Pagans strive to see the very Earth as divine. Many of our rituals embody the value of a sacred world and many of them seek to "heal the Earth" (however this is understood). Many Pagan rituals also focus on experiencing and calling forth the innate divine nature in the participants. There, of course, remains the question of the efficacy of these rites.

In the school of Buddhism called the Great Perfection or Dzog-Chen, this process is taken to its ultimate conclusion, foregoing the transformational quality of Vajrayana. Rather, the Dzog-Chen practitioner seeks the inherent purity in all things, and integrates with the experience while not seeking to change anything about it. This is in accord with the Pagan contra-gnostic view of the immediate goodness of the here and now. In Dzog-Chen this process is said to liberate the practitioner from creating any more karma and eventually lead to the Great Transference in which the body is transformed into pure awareness and light upon death, or in advanced practitioners even before then. Certain deep teachings of the Ceremonialist path speak to this realization, yet it is the distinct failing of the Western path that we have not produced anyone of the caliber of a Tibetan Tulku.

Fortunately we are not finished. If we examine the history of Vajrayana's creation and development as outlined by Miranda Shaw in *Passionate Enlightenment* we can see that the contemporary Pagan movement is in a state very similar to that of the cultural stratum out of which Tantric Buddhism arose and also similar to pre-Buddhist Tibet when Padmasambhava arrived to spread the Dharma.

Unfortunately, the Pagan tradition is floundering and needs a deeper, richer, taproot by which to develop itself beyond mere spellcraft and seasonal celebrations. [See Greer, York, and others for emergent efforts.] When Buddhism escaped the hands of the monastics and attained to the greater view of the Mahayana it began to spread outside the Buddhist philosophical colleges to the villages and craftsfolk. There, among the native magick-using folk of India who were used to honoring the seasons and their many deities, some heard the call of the greater view. They embraced the understanding of the void nature at the ground of things (Shunyata) and saw that compassion (Bodhicitta) was the necessary corollary and result. Rather than give up the magick and methods of worship they had known for countless generations, they brought them to bear on the task of attaining to the complete realization of this View. Thus was born Tantric, Vajrayana Buddhism.

I find it striking that, according to Shaw, it was circles of women seeking buddhahood in feminine form (contrary to the prevailing opinion) that led to this development. They were usually common folk and craftswomen and are accompanied by tales of their enterprising and accomplished skillfulness. They welcomed men into these circles but always with the requirement of the adoration of the feminine as the embodiment of the goal. This is little different from contemporary Pagan circles, whether Gardnerian, Thelemic, Eclectic or Dianic. The automatic authority available to women on the Pagan path is a powerful attraction to women (and men) and one of its deepest strengths.

By understanding that Pagans and Buddhists both cultivate the Bodhisattvic path and share a world view that makes such practice meaningful we can understand how they both can find happiness in innumerable lives in cyclic existence.

Buddhism, like Paganism, has many flavors. In Buddhism they are layered developmentally and any attempt to understand or answer any question depends on which view of Buddhism one is operating from. Interestingly, any particular Buddhist practitioner might choose to speak from any of the three major levels depending of the nature of the question and the querent.

In Hinayana, the first layer, practitioners focus on eliminating the causes of suffering in themselves personally. They withdraw from the world and practice mediation and good behavior until they are enlightened. Mahayana was in part a reaction to the isolation of the monastic life. Its practitioners chose a 'Greater View' that rooted all actions in the dedication to help all beings attain enlightenment, not just the practitioner. This arose from the view prevalent on the Indian subcontinent that all beings incarnate ceaselessly on this world or on others in every variety of form, whether human, animal, spirit or deity. Thus any being you meet, ant, human, or Goddess, may have been formerly your mother (or choose your own preferred relationship), or will be in the future. Being that we are all thus related we should use the care and love that we would have for family and friends to relate to all beings and seek to aid them accordingly.

In Mahayana Buddhism, one who has a thought that has the goal of helping more than the one thinking is having a Bodhisattvic thought. One who dedicates their life, however imperfectly, to the benefit of beings beside one's self, has become a Bodhisattva. The Mahayanists say that this one has truly entered the path towards enlightenment and every act dedicated to the benefit of others helps move the practitioner and all other beings towards enlightenment. When this aspiration becomes an unshakable part of one's being a transformation occurs on the part of the practitioner: they no longer seek enlightenment as a way to escape cyclic existence. They give up the intention to leave behind cyclic existence because in cyclic existence there remain those who still suffer. The Bodhisattva seeks enlightenment in order to be more helpful to beings since the attainment of enlightenment brings with it greater power and skill. The Bodhisattva also chooses to stay in the realm of cyclic existence in order to be where the help is needed.

Tell me, is this not true of every great magick-user we know of in the West, whether as legendary as Merlin or as concrete as the late Scott Cunningham? And do not many of us have this as some measure of our intention as we live our lives and when we work our magicks?

*Thank you, my Husband, but you are being too theoretical. How is this done?*

Very well, My Love, the first step along our journey begins, as you know, with asking for help. Learning to ask for and receive that help is one of the greatest supports on this long road. This practice is similar to a grounding in that it calms and clears us before getting to work. However here we do not simply ground to the planet, rather we ground to what to the planet grounds to, the Ground of Being.

The Buddhists call this kind of practice 'Taking Refuge'. Originally I had a problem with this idea. It seemed to be asking me to leave the field of struggle and go hide somewhere. This seemed wrong to me, even if the hiding place was the lap of the Buddha. But as I mentioned before, a Lama once explained it to me: "Everyone needs help. Refuge is asking for help." So, at the beginning of every practice, we take a moment to ask for help.

We ask for help from three kinds of sources. The most obvious source is the host of enlightened beings like the Buddhas and Bodhisattvas. This includes beings of all classes, Gods, humans, animals and even demons that have attained to enlightenment. Part of this group is also every other being that has vowed to work for the benefit of beings. Some Gods and other spirits have taken this vow and although they have not attained to the supreme enlightenment stand ready to help when asked. They are sometimes called "Those Who Promised." My understanding is that none of these beings will ever force help upon us, although they may wish us well. Instead we must ask for it.

The ultimate source of refuge is the Ground of Being. This 'Ground' is a word-symbol or metaphor that refers to that source out of which all things and all beings arise in the same way as plants arise from the soil. This source is profound, in that there is nothing deeper, powerful, in that everything arises from it, and provident, in that it provides for and supports all things. The Ground of Being is inherently enlightened otherwise enlightenment would not be possible or even a concept. From this ultimate source, the very Ground of Being, we may draw all the resources and help we need. We will be exploring the nature of this 'Ground' along our journey.

The last source of refuge is nearest to home. Even though it is covered up by the muck of our karmas, within us is our already enlightened nature, which through practice we can expose and learn to live in. Regardless of how obscured it is it is always present in us and everyone around us. When we ask for help from this we are asking for help from our own innate enlightenment and that of those we work with and in doing so invite that part of us all to become more manifest. In life it comes flickering through because it is irrepressible. Our challenge is to cultivate it and make it present more and more over time. This practice draws on this awareness and begins the process of cultivation. The method itself is simple:

**Taking Refuge by the 3 Ahs—**
1) Asking for Help
   a) With your eyes open visualize a white capital letter 'A' at your heart.
   b) Take a deep breath and sound a long 'ah'. (Not 'a', and do this whenever you see an 'A' in a practice. We will be doing this often).
   c) Let the vibration center on the letter at your heart and let it radiate light out in all directions. Let the light and sound carry your sincere desire to be helped along the Path.
   d) While sounding and visualizing, imagine the Host of Enlightened Beings and all beings that have vowed to help, your favorite Gods and Spirits, in the space all around you.
   e) Imagine that they hear your 'ah' and turn to face you, as does the enlightened part of you and everyone present, as does the attention of the Ground of Being.

2) Receiving Help
   a) Close your eyes and take another deep breath.
   b) Sound 'ah' and imagine all of those beings lighting up a white letter 'A' at their hearts and as they join you in sounding 'ah', they radiate white light at you (and anyone you are working with). This light fills up your body with 'all good things' and pushes out 'all bad things'. Traditionally this is visualized as white nectar poured into your body through the crown of your head filling it like a vase. All of the 'bad stuff' is pushed out of your body like a black tar or oily smoke, or if you want to be creative (and traditional) poisonous insects, snakes and the like, corresponding to the obstructions in your heart and life.

3) Sharing Help
   a) Having been purified and empowered by the blessing of these beings take a deep breath and open your eyes.

b) Sound 'ah' and visualize the 'A' at your heart again. This time the
Host of Beings sound 'ah' with you and you all radiate white light in
all directions helping all beings that will accept it and wishing all beings well. You can imagine a wave of white light pouring over everyone
you can imagine suffering and being liberated from their hurt and
troubles. The news is a good source of images for this.

Take a week to learn this practice. Do it when you first awake or over cof-
fee or whatever is your morning routine and before you start your day. Do
it again in the middle of your day or when you first come home from work
or school. Do it a third time before going to bed. Do it as slowly as you can.
Later, when you combine this with other practices the investment of time will
pay off. You will have this imbedded deeply enough into your psyche to make
a more rapid pass through it effective. This practice or one like it will open all
ritual and meditative sessions. As you well know, My Love, we also use it to
start all meetings and gatherings. Like the Freemasons say, it is wise to begin
all important undertakings by first invoking the blessing of heaven.

Before we leave the subject of Refuge, My Dear, allow me to quote from
our own Aleister Crowley on the Three Refuges. In his inimitable way Uncle
Al shines a special wisdom on this practice. Please note he spells things differently, drawing from the Pali and not the Sanskrit.

The Three Refuges by Aleister Crowley
(Chapter XII from "Science and Buddhism,"
reprinted in The Collected Works of Aleister Crowley, vol. II, 1906)

Buddham Saranangachami.
Dhammam Saranangachami.
Sangham Saranangachami.
I take my refuge in the Buddha.
I take my refuge in the Dhamma.
I take my refuge in the Sangha.

*This formula of adhesion to Buddhism is daily repeated by countless millions of
humanity; what does it mean? It is no vain profession of reliance on others; no cow-
ardly shirking of burdens—burdens which cannot be shirked. It is a plain estimate of
our auxiliaries in the battle; the cosmic facts on which we may rely, just as a scientist
"relies" on the conservation of energy in making an experiment. Were that principle
of uncertain application, the simplest quantitative experiment would break hopelessly
down. So for the Buddhist.*

I take my refuge in the Buddha.
*That there was once a man who found the Way is my encouragement.*

I take my refuge in the Dhamma.

*The Law underlying phenomena and its unchanging certainty; the Law given by the Buddha to show us the Way, the inevitable tendency to Persistence in Motion or Rest—and Persistence, even in Motion, negates change in consciousness—these observed orders of fact are our bases.*

I take my refuge in the Sangha.

*These are not isolated efforts on my part; although in one sense isolation is eternally perfect and can never be overcome (i.e. on normal planes), in another sense associates are possible and desirable. One third of humanity are Buddhists; add men of Science and we form an absolute majority; among Buddhists a very large proportion have deliberately gone out from social life of any kind to tread these paths of Research.*

*Is the Way very hard? Is the brain tired? The results slow to come? Others are working, failing, struggling, crowned here and there with rare garlands of success. Success for ourselves, success for others; is it not Compassion that binds us closer than all earthlier ties? Aye, in joy and in sorrow, in weakness and in strength, do I take my refuge in the Sangha.*

§

*Distributing or Dedicating the Merit—*

The next practice is to be combined with the first as soon as you are comfortable with Taking Refuge by the 3 Ahs. It will conclude every practice we do and at first will seem counter-intuitive. Yet experience has shown it to be essential if we do not want to be deflected from our goal. It is called 'Dedicating the Merit'.

One of the negative side effects of magickal practice is an inflated ego. Conjuring the powers of the world, conversing with Gods and Angels, transforming ourselves into vast and cosmic beings takes its toll on that part of our psyche that has to moderate the vagaries of our lives in the world. It tends to identify itself with the forces we work with and gets attached to the exalted states we achieve. It starts to think it really is those things and should be treated as such by those around it. To some extent this is true, but the problem is that we get bitchy or giddy or depressed after our practices and this destroys their benefit and generates conflicts with those around us. The Buddhists, having the opportunity to study the effects of their practices for hundreds of years and through many psyches, hit upon an elegant technique for preventing this: giving it all away.

I know it sounds strange, Dear One, to give away the benefit of your hard work, but stay with me on this. When we give it away we dedicate the benefit of our actions to all beings. In the set of all beings is included ourselves. So, in this sense, we are giving away the benefit to ourselves, but not in a generic way. We explicitly dedicate the benefit to help all beings on the path to their release from hurt and their attainment to enlightenment. We are adding to the general thrust of evolution that affects all beings and in so doing align ourselves with that thrust and stand to benefit all the more from it.

The alternative is to try to hang on to the benefit or energy of the work we have done. The problem is that once our attention wavers the energy will collapse into our old patterns and habits that we are trying to change with the practice just completed. If this happens the habit or bad karma will only be ground into us more intensely. It is like trying to hang on to a drop of water by putting it on a plate. Given time, it will evaporate. However, if we put that drop into the ocean of the evolutionary thrust it will be saved and add to that great and beneficent power, so that it has the maximum impact in the world.

It also clears the energy of the practitioners in a manner similar to how we Pagans may touch the Earth at the end of our rites but in a way that preserves the effect and purpose of the rite, not simply discharging excess energy. Some avoid these deleterious effects of ritual by other means. They discharge the energy of the ritual in a "cone of power" or similar technique. If it is discharged there is less or none to cause difficulty. Unfortunately, the energy is rarely put into anything other than the focus of the spell. It could do so much more.

If the energy has been discharged or formed into such a conviviality that extremes of egotistical or self-absorbed emotional discharge are avoided, there remains the subtle after-effect on the ego for having been such a vast and powerful being as a deity. Even when all is said and done, the sense of self importance brought about in our invocations dulls our compassionate acceptance of others and leads us into the errors of judgment that cause harm and dissension; it makes flaming egoists out of us.

What has been presented thus far is only the negative reasons for distributing the benefit of actions. There is a carrot to match this stick. Along with the Buddha-nature present and guiding all beings there is in all of them the desire for happiness and satisfaction. As such this drive has a ubiquitous momentum that can be worked with or against, but can not be ignored. By dedicating the benefit of our actions, particularly our rituals and magick, to the benefit of all beings that they attain to that ultimate happiness and satisfaction called enlightenment, we are tying our magicks into the great stream of evolution, the predominant thrust and momentum in the Universe which, however slowly, moves steadily onward. Our magicks when dedicated to this noble end will be carried along with it to their successful conclusion. Or if they are not actually helpful to the process of benefiting beings they, our magicks, will be simply nullified with a minimum of repercussions.

There is also the added effect that by placing the benefit of actions into the evolutionary stream it is like placing money in a bank where it can not be lost, harmed or destroyed. Once that benefit is given to all beings it will continually have effect on everyone including ourselves. It can not be destroyed by any later negative actions we might perform. It simply adds to the thrust in Being towards the eventual enlightenment of all beings.

**Dedication of Merit—**
Say:
May the benefit of this act and all acts be dedicated
Unto the Complete Liberation and Supreme Enlightenment
Of all Beings everywhere pervading Space and Time, So Mote It Be.

May the benefits of practice, ours and others'
Come to fruition, Ultimately and Immediately
And we remain in the State of Presence—Ah!

The first verse is the general dedication of the merit of our actions. 'Complete Liberation' is a way of referring to the end of suffering. 'Supreme Enlightenment' is a name for that state wherein all of our potentials have been realized. The last line states the focus of our dedication: all beings. In the Buddhist tradition they are referred to as all 'sentient beings' those that possess 'minds'. This is the largest and most all embracing concept of 'mind'. It is everything that feels or reacts to its environment, so perhaps they might use the word 'alive'. This raises the question as to what is alive? Since I have had some very interesting conversations with rocks, machinery, and forces of Nature, I drop the qualifiers and say 'Beings'. In order to point to all of them, the verse invokes the two interpenetrating realms in which all beings dwell, Space and Time, thus covering all places in the past, present and future. It may read like legalese but it is thorough.

The second part is a verse of well-wishing for all practitioners, including one's self. Here we specifically add our energy in support of all who are on the Path. With the last line we enter into the State of Presence, that state where we are in deep communion and contemplation with the world we are in as we sound 'Ah' one last time. While it may take a while to achieve this realization the steady use of it at the end of all practices is very effective. This final 'Ah' is in essence the same as the last 'Ah' in the Refuge practice and the same wave of benefit can be visualized here. Do this daily with Refuge for a week before going on.

*Generating Bodhicitta—*

The third practice to learn completes the set required to produce what the Buddhist ritual masters call "Good at the Beginning, Good in the Middle, Good at the End." We establish good at the beginning by taking refuge and good at the end by dedicating the Merit, but the key to success in practice is good in the middle. This is called Bodhicitta, literally 'Awakened Mind' and translatable as 'Wisdom Attitude.' It is the correct motivation one needs to take in practice to bring about true success.

My Love, Magick without Bodhicitta is Death. If we labor for enlightenment only for ourselves we become ego-bound and ultimately destroy ourselves, yet if we seek the Supreme Enlightenment for the benefit of all beings, attaining to Power so that we may aid those in need, then does the entire Universe conspire to aid us. Please note the strong contrast this makes with Christianity's notion of self-sacrifice. Whereas Christians would expend themselves for others' benefit, the most extreme example being martyrdom, in the Buddhadharma this is understood to reify the belief in a 'self' to offer and thus would lead the practitioner away from enlightenment. The alternative they propose can function regardless of your view of the 'self' existing or not. By simply seeking benefit for all beings, the set of which includes the practitioner, the aspiration helps everyone, and if not immediately then eventually.

The image here is of the practitioner, viewing the plight of innumerable sentient beings adrift in an ocean of suffering, who is moved to want to help them all. When contemplating how to do this, the practitioner realizes that without enlightenment and magickal power little can be done to help them. The practitioner therefore commits themself to assail the rigors of training in the Magickal and Meditative Arts so as to attain to Complete Liberation and the Supreme Enlightenment.

A traditional approach would be making a declaration at this point in the ritual or practice something like:

> There are innumerable beings trapped in suffering
> I vow to save them all
> From now until the realm of suffering is emptied
> I seek enlightenment

There is a thread running through many Pagan rituals, often implicit, that the ritual serves to advance us spiritually. The Tibetan Buddhists make this explicit in all their rituals. They take it further by binding the motivation to seek ultimate spiritual attainment, called generically 'Enlightenment,' to the benefit of all beings. The practitioner seeks enlightenment not merely to be able to escape suffering themselves, but to be able to use the power gained by achieving enlightenment to help all other beings to the same state. This act of generosity is precious in that it benefits many as well as being the only way to attain the supreme realization. It has the added benefit of tying any act or ritual to the thrust of evolution while adding the energy of the ritual to the momentum driving the practitioner towards enlightenment.

But in Thelema and magick we approach a deeper level of practice that operates on not so much of an anthropocentric level but challenges our experience of the world ontologically. Nuit counsels us, "Let there be no difference made among you between any one thing & any other thing for thereby there cometh hurt." (AL1.22)

There is a specific form of Generating Bodhicitta used in the Dzog-Chen tradition of Tibetan Buddhism that is particularly suited for Pagans. It stresses the already-enlightened nature of all beings and makes a commitment to viewing all things in that light. This view was taken when composing a short verse that is said three or more times after Taking Refuge and before beginning the main part of the rite. It is also an attitude to be carried through the entire ritual. As a commitment is being made this verse is sometimes called the 'Vow of Purity'.

**Generating Bodhicitta—**
**Say:**
All is pure and present,
And has always been so.
To this realization
I commit myself—
Pure and Total presence.

This method focuses on the fruit of practice, the realization of the purity and immediate presence of all beings, as the driving force of the practice. When said and intended, practitioners become instantly aware of the extent to which they do not actually perceive all phenomenon as pure and present. This contrast generates a powerful thrust towards the realization of that state which can then be used in the subsequent ritual practice. By recognizing that this state of purity and presence applies to all beings, the force that is generated includes the motivation to bring all beings to this same awareness.

Although you are learning it third, it is to be done between Refuge and the Dedication of Merit. Again, do this for a week before going on.

*About Modalities—*
Before we go on, a word about 'visualization'. There are many modalities through which we perceive and interact with the world: vision, hearing, touch, smell, taste and thought. Most of us process the world and remember our experiences primarily through one of these, though another may be a strong second. To figure this out in your case ask yourself how you remember experiences. Do you have an image in your mind, or do you remember what everyone said? The first would be a visual memory, the latter auditory. Also ask how you solve problems. Do you visualize a solution or talk it through, or do you 'feel it out'? The first is visual again (this is the dominant mode in our culture), talk is aural, the last is tactile. Some folk sniff out problems, and I'm sure that somebody out there can taste the solution, though I've never met them. Pure cognition without sensory reference would be the thought modality, but this is the realm of the noetic and we will leave that for another discussion.

The reason for bringing this up is that 'visualization' in the sense of seeing the phases of a practice is not the only way to get the job done. Sound and touch are also just as effective. For instance, the Tibetans tend to focus on the visual while the Vedic tradition is auditory. I'm sure the other senses could be used as well. However, in writing this, I can't always refer to all of the modalities. So when I say 'visualize' know that you should use the modality that works for you. As an example I don't really visualize pentagrams when I draw them. I feel them as a diamond-like density in space before me, invisible but functioning in exactly same way as a blazing image of one. Similarly in the Refuge practice, I feel the waves of energy passing into me and over the world with the vibration of the sound I'm making, more than see them.

When there is some special value in it I will refer to the variations in the practices that the modalities expose. Sometimes practices demand the use of a specific modality because the action is being done with one of them. In these cases do your best. It will strengthen your sub-dominant modality. The rest of the time, translate the practice into your strength, as you need to.

# 3

# Empowerment & Uniting with the Teacher

Beloved, one of the great conflicts or challenges in interfacing Buddhism, particularly Vajrayana, with contemporary Paganism, and especially Thelema, is the attitude to take towards the Guru. In all of the literature about the practice of tantra the relationship with the Guru or teacher is paramount. After having suitably tested the individual one hopes to have as one's teacher, the student is to unreservedly devote themself to the teacher. This includes doing what they say, serving their personal needs, prostrations and other signs of deference, and in the exalted stages of tantra viewing the teacher as a Buddha in body, speech, and mind. Unfortunately, this runs exactly counter to Pagan culture, attitudes and even ethics or morals.

Pagans are fiercely independent. Thelema has the injunction to "bend not the knee" to any power, human, divine or other. The closest thing we have to the Guru relationship comes through the value some Pagans place on initiatory lineage. Yet, even in these cases the devotion to a living person never achieves the same degree of intensity as the Guru relationship, particularly as a cultural norm.

There are certain advantages to the Guru relationship. The practice is founded on the idea that the Guru has already attained in some real measure if not completely to enlightenment. Thus they are qualified to show the student how to get there. If I could find an obviously and truly enlightened Pagan I might feel the same way about them, but none have crossed my path. The process of serving the teacher is a direct way of rebalancing the energy the teacher expends toward the student's development while also freeing up the teacher for doing the task of teaching. Prostrations have the excellent effect of beating down ego and pride into something less of a distraction and more of a help. Also, prostrations place the student in a 'yin' state making it easier to receive from the teacher and the practices.

Viewing the teacher as a Buddha, the most extreme form of this relationship, is rooted in a discovery by the practitioners that has more to do with the aspiration of the student than the attainment of the teacher. It uses the psychological power of projection, which will come into play regardless simply due to the fact of the interpersonal relationship with the one who is the teacher. Rather than letting this arise out of our neuroses, we are counseled to see the teacher as a Buddha, their speech as teaching, their actions as compassionate, their associates as the retinue of a Buddha, and so forth. While this has the effect of placing the student continually in the 'presence of the sacred', itself profound, the practitioners point to an even more determinant quality with respect to the student's development. As they put it, if one views the teacher as an ordinary person the attainment received is that of an ordinary person, if one views the teacher as a Buddha the attainment is that of a Buddha, and if one views the teacher as a small dog, the attainment is that of a small dog.

Aside from such strategies as taking transmission from qualified Tibetan Lamas, Pagans do not have access to such beings as true Gurus. Yet, in addition to some truly excellent teachers with whom the Guru relationship does not apply, there is another approach that can serve the same purpose. It is not as easy as actually having a person in front of you helping, guiding, and teaching. Instead it is rooted in the fact that within each and every being there lies the 'Tathagatagarbha', the bornless Buddha-nature, that is driving (or luring) everything unto its complete liberation and supreme enlightenment. However buried in each being the Tathagatagarbha is it can be related to by the practitioner as a manifestation of the Guru. In fact, it is a manifestation of the ultimate Guru even in the view of the Lamas, who see that teaching-nature as inherently present in all beings, and whom ultimately we must rely on. The Western Adepts know this as the 'Holy Guardian Angel' or 'Genius' or 'Daemon,' or 'Bornless One,' the inner teacher who guides our magickal education.

When it comes to practice it is not enough to maintain a good attitude towards the teacher. During our practice the goal is to unite with the teacher so as to achieve their attainment to whatever extent you are capable. This is called Empowerment and is a more developed form of the second 'A' in the Refuge Practice. We take empowerment near the beginning of our practice, after asking for help (Refuge), and getting into the right frame of mind (Bodhicitta). We ask for and receive blessing from the Teacher and then unite with the Teacher that we may wield their same power in our practice. There are several ways we can do this, only two of which we will cover now. Give them no less than a week's practice if you expect results.

As we discussed previously, My Dear, in Thelema we can view Hadit, "the flame that burns in every heart of man, and in the core of every star," as

Tathagatagarbha and so a very direct mode of empowerment can be found in a 'non-invocation' ["'Come unto me' is a foolish word for it is I that go."] imaged as the Winged Globe (AL2.6-7):

## Empowerment by Hadit—

**First,** center in your heart, which you imagine as a golden Winged Globe. Using breath, sound 'Ah,' golden light, tactile feeling, or simply pure devotion and ardent prayer-intent, radiate outward your request for empowerment throughout the Cosmos.

**Next,** all of the Teachers throughout existence, even the Cosmos Itself, hear your plea and on the reflux or inhale, or whatever suits your modality, force comes flooding back into your heart and the Winged Globe brightens with power and shines throughout your being, strengthening you.

*This also has a higher arc for those with the necessary capacity. As autogenesis and cosmogenesis are iterative and inalienably entwined, we know that in each moment's concrescent realization the Cosmos makes us and we make the Cosmos. With each iteration of this empowerment we have the opportunity to take power from the Cosmos as It makes us and to recognize It as our own creation as we make It. Praise be to All the Gods for Creation, unfinished!*

**Repeat** the cycle until you are satisfied.

This process can be developed even further when we apply it to an anthropomorphic teacher. When the teacher is something human-like, we can see them as possessing chakras and take our empowerment therefrom. In Thelema Ra-Hoor-Khuit is the Lord of Initiation and therefore the Hierophant and Teacher, and can help us in this capacity.

## Empowerment by Ra-Hoor-Khuit—

**First** invoke or at least imagine Ra-Hoor-Khuit before you and facing you. For example, you can use the image on the Aeon card in the Thoth Tarot deck. You may wish to use associated verses or songs to conjure Him.

**Next,** once the visualization is together, create 'connection points' at the chakras with colored spheres. Classically only the brow (white), throat (red) and heart (blue) chakras are used to represent and empower Body, Speech and Mind respectively, but you can use as many as you like. You can use sounds here as well: the syllables we will use later are respectively Had, Re (*ray*), and Nu (*new*). You can begin using them now (see illustration in chapter 6).

**Then,** reach out with your hands and draw one sphere at a time toward the same point on your body. Let it trail a ribbon or ray of color from the body of the Teacher towards yours. Feel the empowerment associated with that chakra flood that aspect of your being.

**Once** all of Ra-Hoor-Khuit's chakras are connected with your own, sound 'Ah'. Imagine Him dissolving from back to front until only the chakras are left. **Finally,** imagine they come towards and unite with the chakras of your body. This unites you with the Teacher so that you are of 'one taste'. Rest.

My Love, at advanced levels of practice, we can also take this even further. The magi possess a formula for accessing this profound aid universally. This is to be found in the vow of the Magister Templi; "I vow to perceive every phenomenon as the direct communication between God and my soul." If we take 'God' here as the teacher, the Guru, and treat every action of the 'Guru', in the tantric manner, as 'Buddha', one can find one's self continually in the presence of the Guru and continually receiving teaching. Every person, animal, plant, event, object and so on becomes the teacher and source of teachings. Everything good, bad or indifferent becomes an aid on the path to enlightenment. And when it becomes uncertain what the teacher is trying to get across it is also helpful to remember that the teacher is also a trickster.

# 4

# The Two Accumulations

This work, Dear One, has much the character of a linear accelerator. Each step adds more power or thrust so we can take the next step, which in turn adds more strength to the working. So, before we go leaping ahead into the deity invocation before us, we take a brief detour to gather yet more power.

Whereas before we first sought power from Those Who Promised, the sources of Refuge, then we put ourselves in right alignment with the evolutionary thrust of being, the Cosmos' own drive to awaken all within it. Next we turned to the Teacher for empowerment and blessing where the three dimensions of our being, Body, Speech, and Mind, are energized for the work ahead. Now we will gather two kinds of our own power and put them to use to make the leap into the invocation of the Deity.

The first kind of power is our own Karma, specifically our Merit or 'good karma'. Duly empowered and blessed, we perform an act of power and bless all beings with four immeasurable goodnesses. By doing good in this way it puts us in touch with all the other good we have done, which can be said to amount to variations on the four blessings we are giving. Action (the meaning of the word Karma) lets us grasp the causal chains that bind all things together and use their inexorable process to drive our ascent to Divine presence.

The second kind of power is called Wisdom and is measured by our capacity to recognize the void nature of the Ground of Being out of which all phenomena arise and to which they all return. At first this tends to be minimal, but with practice that spaciousness becomes our primary resource from which to create.

So, My Dear, by taking up your karma and applying your wisdom you will be able to assay the great task of calling before you the presence of a God. Being one of the supreme human tasks, you will need all the help you can get. Let us explore each of these accumulations in turn.

*The Four Immeasurables*
The Four Immeasurables are four blessings we can pour out into the world in an act of profound magick that benefits all beings. Because of the infinite possibilities for good that dwell in such a profound blessing they are each called 'immeasurable.'

We in turn are benefited twice. First by so blessing ourselves, but also, as mentioned above, we connect with and gather up all our meritorious karma and use it to add to our strength to invoke the Divine.

To begin, you will imagine at your heart a white letter 'A' as you did before. Love, we will be doing this and its kin a lot in our practices. By building on this single skill we develop great capacity to wield power this way.

Very much like the radiating of a general blessing as you did in taking Refuge, you will now radiate a specific blessing to specific classes of beings. Who you start with depends on your current state of mind. If you do not have a clear sense of self-love, compassion for yourself and a general sense of well-being, start with directing the radiance in the following practice towards yourself. If you do not have this established from the start you will not have a basis with which to do this for others. Once this is established you can skip over yourself if you wish and direct your efforts towards others, but it is never wrong to strengthen yourself this way too.

These are the objects of this practice:
1) Ourselves (if we need it),
2) Those we know intimately, our family and friends as well as our enemies or those we are in conflict with,
3) Next those we are connected to but not intimate with, such as people we work with, but not closely.
4) Then those we have heard of, or can imagine like people in the news or animals and life throughout the planet or the cosmos,
5) and finally objectless radiance, shining out as does a star.

For each of the next following steps we radiate a specific energy towards each of these recipients in turn.

**Irrespective of our object, we start with** *loving-kindness*. Radiate the warm soft feelings of love, kindness, and the spontaneous affection that you experience when seeing a small child, a kitten, or a puppy. Beam this as white light pouring out in all directions (or towards and filling yourself) from the 'A' in your heart while sounding 'Ah' with the first breath. If the feeling is vague repeat this as many times as you need to for the feeling to become clear, steady and as strong as you can manage.

**Next** we notice that these beings that we care for hurt. So now we sound 'Ah' and shine white light again, as many times as necessary, radiating *compassion*, which is the will to relieve suffering. For each of the objects of our attention we imagine them being liberated from their sufferings and oppressions as the wave of our light passes over and through them. Imagine them being lifted up out of the mire, being healed, being freed, all of their obstacles cleared, every deficiency filled.

**Next,** we radiate again, but this time focusing on the *joy* the recipients of our blessings experience from being liberated from their suffering. And we feel joy with them. To make this as strong as possible, imagine the objects of your attention entering the most extreme state of joy: enlightenment.

**Lastly,** we sound 'Ah' again, and this time, lest they be distracted, we establish all beings in the calm abiding of *equanimity*. This tempers the joy and stabilizes it into happiness.

Having done this round for your first object, perhaps yourself, **next** direct it towards all the people you know, with whom you have personal connection like family or friends, and the other people you know personally like those you are in conflict with, or work closely with.

**Sound the 'Ah's again,** and send it to anyone you have ever heard of. I think of this as 'the people in the news', the good, the bad, and the ugly in the world who, mostly, are hurting. You do not need to limit this to humans. Direct your loving kindness toward all of the animals and other creatures of this world or any other you can imagine. Imagine them being washed with your blessing and feeling that support.

**Finally, Sound the round of the Four Immeasurables again,** and simply radiate out the blessing without an object like a star that radiates light and heat without regard to who receives it. Ultimately, this is the state we strive to achieve all of the time.

As you can now see, I'm sure, My Love, each of the Four Immeasurables, Loving-kindness, Compassion, Joy in the joy of others and Equanimity, flow from the preceding. This is because each one is an antidote for the potential disability of the radiance that came before.

Loving-kindness can degenerate into maudlin sentimentality, so we temper it with compassion, the deep awareness of suffering and will to end it. But, that very compassion can be depressing and lead to melancholy. So, we temper it with joy in the joy of those we help. However, joy can degenerate into a giddiness that detracts from pleasure and presence both, so we temper it with equanimity. Yet equanimity can lead to a detached coldness so it is tempered by engaging with loving-kindness. Thus do we turn this wheel of blessing.

You will also find that after having gone this round of 16 or 20 Ah's you have conjured the provident power of existence itself. Take a moment to feel this course through you. This is the first accumulation.

Below is the practice in summary. Be sure to learn the detail of the practice above before using it. Add it in to your daily work for a week, at least.

**The Four Immeasurables—**
**Sound (4, 16, or 20x):**
A—  *Awaken Loving Kindness–Compassion–Joy in their Joy–Equanimity*
   *Toward:*
   *Yourself–All who are close to you–All who are connected to you–*
   *All who you know of–To the non-objectified All*

*Entering the Ground—*
   My Love, "Nothing is a secret key of this law" (AL1.46). In the Buddhadharma, the knowledge of the Void and the Void-nature of all things is reckoned 'wisdom'. We who follow in the footsteps of the Ancients are 'Lovers of Wisdom' or Philosophers. Thus it is that we cultivate our relationship with Nuit, to love Whom is "better than all things."
   Qabalah, Thelema, the Buddhadharma, Parmenides, and certain branches of physics today all posit a medium out of which phenomena arise. That medium, called variously full (Pleroma) or empty (Vacuum), is void of characteristics that would render it sensible to us. Had it any such characteristics it would be unable to produce all phenomena. Yet it is full of all form, as every form comes from this source. As such, some call it the Ground.
   To borrow a perspective from geometry as an aid to understanding, if we reckon that the Ground contains each individual form, then every form must be accompanied by its opposite. When we contemplate adding together each form and its opposite we realize quickly we are imagining a space that is hyper-symmetric until we reach the super-symmetry of the space some physicists say existed 'before' the Big-Bang.
   The Buddhadharma understands that the realization of the Ground is the attainment of wisdom since understanding that Void teaches us the nature of all things in their unity and diversity, in their impermanence and eternality. The supreme realization of this brings the liberation that is enlightenment, but most of us have a long way to go to achieve it. Fortunately, the process itself brings many benefits along the way before we fully attain.
   In the Mahayana tradition of the Buddhadharma some of the fundamental principles of practice and experience take on anthropomorphic form. This lets the practitioner better identify with that principle. The text that declares the fundamental conundrum of the Ground as Void is the Prajñaparamita Sutra, sometimes called the Heart Sutra, heart as the core of the matter. This sutra takes on embodiment as the Buddha-Goddess Prajñaparamita who is invoked as the embodiment of the wisdom aspect of the ground of being to teach the practitioner the truth about the sheer openness of the Ground. She is also called the Mother of all Buddhas.
   We find a startling parallel in Thelema with Nuit. In the first Chapter of Liber AL, Nuit presents herself as Infinite Space, with all that it contains, and as the desirable consort of practice. In every attempt to reify her she yet turns into the None, the Not, sheer space and with it bliss, light, and knowledge. This is what we are to desire and seek. Shortly, My Dear, we will do so.

To do this we immerse ourselves in the Void, the omnipresent Body of Nuit as the Thelemites call it. The Buddhists call it formally (amongst other things) Shunyata, which is often translated as 'void' or 'emptiness' or more modernly 'openness'. My favorite translation comes from H.V. Guenther who expressed it as "the sphere whose center is everywhere and its circumference is nowhere". This phrase has a venerable pedigree beginning with "God is a circle whose center is everywhere, and its circumference nowhere." —Empedocles (495-435 B.C.). For St. Bonaventura, 1221-74 C.E., in *The Mind's Road to God*, 'being' is experienced as "an intelligible sphere whose center is everywhere and whose circumference is nowhere." More recently "Nature is an infinite sphere of which the center is everywhere and the circumference nowhere,"—Blaise Pascal, *Pensées*, 1670. Thelemites will refer to AL2.3.

As we gain familiarity with the Ground, we can access it progressively more effectively. Once we have a clear grasp of it two great powers become available to us: the ability to draw desired [divine] forms from It and the ability to liberate forms from one manifestation into an other, more desired, form, or into no form at all. The first is the art of Symbolic Recreation and the latter is called 'Self-Liberation'.

Our first step is to find the Ground. It is a truism in teaching that the obvious is the hardest to point to, so a story here may help, Dear One. In India, one of the traditional ways of engaging with a Teacher is to ask the same question every time you meet. I presume that this is to deepen the question with the attainment of the student, but I can also see how this might be annoying. So it was when a wealthy student was asking his Guru for the umpteenth time, "What is meditation?" In a fit of pique, the Guru responded succinctly, "Between your thoughts there is space, attend to that space and make it longer. This is meditation."

Start here, My Love, or you will be trapped in discursive thought and the true magick of this way will be unavailable to you.

As you practice your mind will quiet and more profound creativity will emerge. Confronted with problems or puzzles, or the need to make decisions, when you still your mind the solution or 'way through' will spring to mind. All freedom comes from space. At this juncture we discover that the space has been cluttered by our thoughts. When we stop proliferating them, a new view of the mind becomes visible.

The difference is much like day and night, quite literally. In normal thought we experience the mind much like the day-lit sky, brightly filled with objects, a blue sky: the brilliant sun of discursive awareness. Yet when the sun of the talking self finally sets, we see the sky for what it truly is, an ocean infinitely deep of self-luminous stars. There is so much more to the world than we can see while talking to ourselves.

Besides the contemplations given above, there is a practice that invokes the promise made by Nuit to us all to know Her, She who embodies the Ground. This is one of the blessings of Thelema, Dearest, that as we can find the Star in every individual, so can we find the Teacher in the Ground from which the stars arise embodied as Nuit (it is Her knowledge after all —AL1.32).

In the practice, Dear One, we first call upon Nuit through a dramatic group of verses from the Book of the Law that set the relationship we are to have with Nuit and describe the process we will then cultivate. In cultivating the empowerment we progressively dissolve the four manifest elements into Space itself and ourselves along with them. At the end there is only Space, Our Lady of the Night.

The initial verses of the first two Chapters set the stage. We'll discuss this more later, but for now let the incantatory quality of these phrases carry you. Speak the words in roman type; *the italic gives directions.*

### Entering into the Ground of Nuit—
*After taking Refuge and generating Bodhicitta. . .*
Say:
Had! The manifestation of Nuit. *And the Winged Globe appears*
Nu! the hiding of Hadit.          *And the O'er-arching Woman appears*
   *Then we invoke Her promise to us all. If you require words...*
Say:
Oh Nuit! By the vault of Your body; by Your sacred heart and tongue; by all You can give, by all You desire of us all, I invoke your adamantine Vow, Let the joys of Your love redeem us from all pain.

*The following incantation sets the tone of the practice, articulates the cosmology and invokes the Lady as the embodiment of the attainment as the Teacher. Success is marked by the experience of the "dew of her light bathing" you. This is the anointing that initiates and consecrates kings, priests and magi alike. When it pours forth on you let it dissolve you.*
Say:
Who am I and what shall be the sign? So she answered him, bending down, a lambent flame of blue, all touching, all penetrant, her lovely hands upon the black earth, & her lithe body arched for love, and her soft feet not hurting the little flowers:

Thou knowest! And the sign shall be my ecstasy, the consciousness of the continuity of existence, the omnipresence of my body [the unfragmentary non-atomic fact of my universality*].

Then the priest answered & said unto the Queen of Space, kissing her lovely brows, and the dew of her light bathing his whole body in a sweet-smelling perfume of sweat: *(feel it pour upon you)*
Say:
O Nuit, continuous one of Heaven, let it be ever thus; that men speak not of Thee as One but as None; and let them speak not of thee at all, since thou art continuous!

**Say (hearing Her answer):**
None, breathed the light, faint & faery, of the stars, and two. For I am divided for love's sake, for the chance of union. This is the creation of the world, that the pain of division is as nothing, and the joy of dissolution all. *Be anointed with the Kisses of Nuit.*

*To be thorough we cycle through the elements in the reverse Vedic order, that is (roughly) in decreasing density, dissolving each of them in turn, in order to dissolve it all. The subjective form is Bliss, the Mind still and clear. See also the seventh chapter of Liber Ararita.*

**Sound:**

| | |
|---|---|
| AL—*Transform into earth* | *Be anointed with the Kisses of Nuit* |
| NU—*Dissolve into water* | *Be anointed with the Kisses of Nuit* |
| RE—*Ignite into fire* | *Be anointed with the Kisses of Nuit* |
| HAD—*Dissipate into air* | *Be anointed with the Kisses of Nuit* |
| Ah—*Unfold into space* | *Be anointed with the Kisses of Nuit* |

{*Please see the manuscript of Liber AL. Sadly, Crowley did not understand what Nuit was saying and balked. It refers to all that is not entitative, everything not Hadit. This line, struck from the typeset version, can here be used at your discretion.}

While sounding the seed syllable of each element invoke the presence of Nuit and feel her 'dew' pouring out upon you dissolving each element in turn. Imagine yourself as a human with the incantation, then as stone or earth as you sound 'AL'. With 'NU' (*new*) dissolve the earth into a pure liquor of water. With 'RE' (*ray*), like ignited alcohol let the water burn until there is only fire. With 'HAD' let the fire dissipate and cool into moving air. Then with the final 'Ah' let the very molecules of the air you imagine yourself to be unfurl into the space from which they arise. Rest here. You can also repeat this as often as necessary to achieve the desired result.

Darling, practice this once to thrice daily for a week until you can comfortably dissolve into Her embrace and rest there without chasing after your thoughts and feelings.

The purpose of this practice is to cultivate skills and capacities that will be required of you on this path. The first is the ability to take empowerment in yet a third way, to ask for and receive help. The second is the capacity to rest in sheer Openness which is the Ground out of which All arises. This fundamental ability will be used extensively in the practices ahead. And third, on a very different scale, it introduces you to a set of seed syllables that, due to their attributes, are used again in other rites and develops the skill in their use.

*Self-Liberation*

Dearest, one of the most useful practices to come out of the Dzog-Chen community in the Buddhadharma, through taking the view of the Ground as sheer openness, is the process of self-liberation. Let us explore the nature of the process and a method for employing it.

Have you ever been having a great time, riding high on good feelings when bad news comes and bums you out? Or the inverse of this—being depressed when suddenly something happens that lifts your spirits? In that moment of change you experienced the phenomenon of liberation. What makes it self-liberation is when you can do this intentionally. What is going on is that since all forms are essentially openness, liberating a feeling, a thought, or a sensation is returning it to that open state. When this happened as above, when your mood was dashed or lifted, the mood that passed was opened out while the new mood arose in your consciousness. When you do this intentionally, there is no need to replace the old state with a new one. Rather, you permit your awareness to return to its natural uncontrived state which is content-free, lucent and joyous.

This is the most important notion in the process of self-liberation. What we are being liberated from is the contents of our consciousness. Not that we are striving to not think or feel or sense, but rather that we do not grasp after our thoughts, etc., distracting ourselves from what is going on, or Qabalistically speaking, getting caught up in our Netzachian dreams. What we are being liberated into is the experience of the mind in its true nature, which is content-free, thus open; unclouded by form, thus radiant; not clinging, thus feeling pleasure. This state of pleasure-radiance-openness is both the goal and the guide to the process of self-liberation. This tripartite state is actually one thing but when experienced through the human mind, we divide its unitary, non-dual nature into the three characteristics of pleasure, radiance, and openness which correspond to the three parts of embodied existence, body, speech (or energy) and mind, respectively.

To get there we need to learn to relax, but we need to understand how. The Tibetans talk about this in terms of View, Meditation, and Action. First, we must understand the View. Here the View is the understanding that the nature of the mind is pleasure-radiance-openness. Given that hypothesis we then practice experiencing this state through Meditative techniques. Lastly, once the View has been stabilized through Meditative practice, which is to say that you have convinced yourself of the View experientially, it is then put into Action by applying the technique learned in meditation in life outside of meditative practice.

So, for the moment I must ask you to accept the working hypothesis that the nature of the mind is pleasure-radiance-openness so that we can create an experimental design that can help us verify the theory, i.e., a meditative practice. First, unless you are a Buddha, one who dwells permanently in the state of pure pleasure-radiance-openness, there will be in your body some degree of displeasure or pain; in your speech some impediment to your expression, or said in another way, one very accessible to a magick-user like yourself, some block to your energy; in your mind some thought that is not passing away, even if it is only your thoughts about this teaching. Which ever is the strongest or most immediate put your attention there. Whatever it is that you are attending to, give it room. If it is a physical sensation or emotional feeling, relax around it, let it dissipate and dilute itself across a wider area, losing its intensity. If it is a block in your energy, let it unravel like a knot being loosed. If it is a thought, let it dissolve into sheer openness.

At this stage of practice, you may not be able to make the focus of your attention to completely dissipate the "object," particularly if it is strong physical pain. But to the extent that you have been successful in liberating some small bit of either body, energy or mind, notice that you also feel some increase in the other two qualities. If you liberated a thought, notice the increase of pleasure in your body and radiance in your energy. If you focused on a knot in your energy, notice the increase in the expansive peace in your mind and the added pleasure in your body. If it was sensation that you liberated, note your increased energy and clarity of mind.

Keep practicing this. Every time you do this round you will feel better, have more energy and greater mental lucidity. You also develop greater capacity for doing this, and are able to liberate progressively greater portions of the focus of your attention into its true nature. Anything that is not pleasure or radiance or openness is at the same time closedness of mind, dimming of energy, and dulling or paining of sensation. When unfurled like a flower blooming, all three qualities are strengthened.

When I do this I go into whatever happens to be most immediate to me, whether a sensation or my energy or my mind and crank it open. As the other two qualities collaterally increase, I may shift my attention to wherever the next strongest block appears, and liberate that bit of clinging, and then on to the next item that comes up. As I do this my mind becomes clearer, my energy stronger, my sense of pleasure and well-being becomes greater. I follow this trail of liberation until I am in the state of lucent radiant bliss, as much as I can stand at the time. It gets better the more I do this, as my capacity for pleasure, free energy, and open-mindedness increases.

Dzog-Chen teaches that this process of self-liberation has three stages of development. First one must attend to the phenomenon as to be liberated and exert effort to liberate it. With increased capacity, the process of liberation becomes effortless, but still requires attention to the process for it to work. Finally, the act of liberating the phenomenon arises at the same moment as the phenomenon, spontaneously, liberating it. This last stage is Self-Liberation, as each phenomenon liberates itself.

# 5

# The Why and What of Deity Yoga

Sweet One, Deity Yoga is the art of making present the characteristic nature and virtue or power of a Deity. It is the basis of worship in all theistic religions and has powerful applications in personal evolution and magickal practice. Although our focus is on knowing the Thelemic God Ra-Hoor-Khuit, the principles of deity invocation, worship, and union can be applied generally.

Although this is not the place to make the argument, it can be said that the practice of uniting with a Deity is the central practice and core secret to all magick. Humans have limited magickal power on their own. We can cause change, but by being at the bottom of the divine chain of being, there is only so much we can do on our own. Yet by being of the Divine, albeit the least, and by being holons and thus microcosms of the Cosmos itself, we have the essence of all of the Gods within us. By cultivating our awareness of those divine seeds and activating them through the proper processes we can gain the benefit of their natures and wield their powers. The most important of these benefits is that we are drawn further up the chain of being towards the Absolute, or subjectively, Enlightenment.

One obvious benefit of practicing Deity Yoga is that you get to meet the Gods. Manifesting in unspeakable variety, contact with the realm of the Gods ends doubt as to whether the Gods are 'real'. We may spend the rest of our lives contemplating the nature of these vast, ancient and powerful beings, but once you have been touched by the unmistakable presence of a Deity you know it the same as you know the taste of sugar. No one can convince you that sugar does not exist. Some come by the experience spontaneously while others need more direct help and attention. For instance, someone already in contact with the God can mediate or bestow the experience. It is also possible to perform practices without the help of an introduction and eventually make contact. This is naturally harder, but by no means impossible. If one's karma is right, it can in fact be very quick.

Being touched by a Deity makes a permanent change in the person so touched. Once the Realm of the Gods makes the connection to you the lines of communication can flow both ways. Also, there is always the possibility that communication from Deities other than the One Who touched you can be initiated. Over the years I have met a number of people who have had such experiences where they unequivocally met a Deity. It changed their lives and often made them priestfolk. While this contact is not entirely necessary to enter the priesthood those who have it are marked. I refer to them as the 'God-touched'.

It may come as a surprise that Deities are not actually necessary for Deity Yoga. A practitioner upon (and by) their attainment to enlightenment can create a form that remains in the world and can be used by subsequent practitioners as a method to further their own evolution. (Some, however, may argue that the enlightened practitioner has become a god and so this is not a special case.) Deities, by being Deities, do the same thing, creating what is called a 'godform'. This is their characteristic mode of presentation, or at least one of them, and is used in their worship and invocation. The godform is visualized and the Deity comes to inhabit and animate the form.

It is important to recognize that Deities are in a real sense transcendent of the form we see Them in. When we visualize a form and invite a Deity to inhabit it, we are giving Them a vehicle through which to express Themselves, making it easier to communicate with us, but Their presented form is not Their 'true' form. As the Greek myth of Semele warns us, it may be very dangerous to see a God's true form. It is said that this is why the Egyptians drew their deities in profile. Some of the Deity is visible in the form and some, perhaps most of the Deity, is always beyond our ken. We must remember that They are forever mysteries.

The relevant part here is that what works as a vehicle for Them, works as a vehicle for us too. With or without the presence of the actual Deity the form still possesses Its characteristics and attributes (the personality and the powers). We can take on the form of the Deity, or of the ascended practitioner, and use it on our path.

This is not some crass acquisition of power for power's sake. Each and every one of us is up against what has been called by philosophers the 'Problem Situation'. This is literally the challenge that is our lives. We all are faced with the demands of the body, of society, and of our desire to improve our condition. The magickal path is the road to 'divinizing' ourselves through the acquisition of magickal power and knowledge. The details as to what this means I will leave up to your theology. Regardless of interpretation one method is through taking on a godform and learning to see the world through the 'view' of that God and learning to wield Its attributes. The difficulty in doing this drives the motivation to pick a Deity to work with primarily or even exclusively. Practice here, like elsewhere, makes perfect.

Nor is this process entirely self-centered, My Love. I've heard it said that if you do not acquire magickal power before becoming a Buddha, when you do you will be useless for helping other beings. This wise attitude must be our primary motivation.

## Worship

Besides being a subjective point of view Deities also embody a way of living in society. Hera, for example, embodies the virtues of marriage; Hermes is the embodiment of commerce. When we work with these Gods we strengthen their virtues in our lives and in the lives of those around us.

Traditionally the way to do this is called 'worship'. This word derives from the Old Saxon and with a slight shifting of the vowels we discover the etymology: 'worth-shaping'. Worship is the process of giving shape to the values that the Deities we worship embody. When we use the means of worship, namely invocation, ritual and offerings, we make present the 'spirit' or essential character of the Deity. This impresses upon us, and our world, Their distinct nature and way of doing things. The Deities worshiped in a stable and traditional society embodied the values and ways of life in that culture. The rituals conveyed those values from generation to generation. This is an ancient and venerable means for holding a society together, on the order of 30,000 years old.

## Why you should not do Deity Yoga

Deity Yoga is not without risks. The principal ones are obsession, overshadowing, and dependency.

The presence of a Deity can be one the of most awesome and pleasurable experiences of a lifetime. Sometimes the human mind grasps onto such a presence with such tenacity that it refuses to let go. The Deity becomes the obsessive focus of attention such that the duties of life become neglected. While on retreat this may be acceptable, when trying to do one's job or caring for the children this is pathological and needs to be avoided.

Sometimes it is the Deity Who has trouble letting go of the aspirant, in which case the Deity does not quite ever go away after dismissal. The Deity can lurk just beyond the firelight circle of conscious awareness influencing the choices of the practitioner. It is important to learn how to note if one of the Great Old Ones is overstaying its welcome and how to politely send It on Its way.

Usually the two problems above are derived from the third, dependency. With a few notable exceptions, is it important to develop yourself first before working with Deities. Someone who has not done their clearing work with the Lesser Banishing Ritual of the Pentagram (or its equivalents), learned to raise their own energy with something like the Middle Pillar, and and awaken to their wholeness by such practices as conjuring the Elemental and Planetary powers on their own is vulnerable to the temptation to take a shortcut. When you work with a Deity their presence and powers wrap around you and support you. If you already have power of your own this Divine power augments and extends yours. If you don't, i.e., if you have not done your own work (without the aid of a Deity) and successfully acquired the powers of the Elements and the Planets, and so on, having a Deity's power available to you will make it feel as though you have done the work. However, when the Deity is not present, the power is gone too.

One result of this is that you may become obsessed with the presence of the Deity, which is problematic as mentioned above. On the other hand the Deity may decide you are a pushover and try to take over your life. If you have done your work and have your own power base, you have the ability to argue most potently against the unwanted overshadowing. The moral of this lesson is: acquire your own power. Besides, it makes you a much better ally of the Deity.

As with many things in life there is an exception to this. A number of Deities are specifically anagogic in their character and this is why in some traditions They are engaged from the beginning. In the Tibetan tradition of Deity Yoga, after suitable preliminaries, one turns one's attention to the invocation of a Yi-dam, a word which means literally 'mind-protector' but is often translated for its religious function as 'tutelary deity'. It is common that for a given school or tradition a singular Deity serves this function for most if not all practitioners in it. Ra-Hoor-Khuit is one such.

Like in the Tibetan case, Ra-Hoor-Khuit is the embodiment of the path and success on it. He is both vehicle and resultant, and so practitioners on the Thelemic Way may take on His form and thereby come to know, embody and wield their pure will. The practice before us is one way to achieve this. Due to this reflexive quality, by taking on His form our own wills are purified and strengthened, so there is no concern for obsession, overshadowing, and dependency. Nonetheless, the preliminaries of the Western practice outlined above both prepare one for the Divine presence and develop the skills that make such conjuration easier.

# 6

# The Maha Yoga Tantra Invocation of Ra-Hoor-Khuit

Beloved, now that we have developed some skills and capacities, and perhaps some understanding, we can at last turn to the core method of all magickal practice, especially tantra: invoking the Gods. The method given here is a version of that same practice alluded to in the Asclepius (v24) of the Hermetic Corpus wherein a spirit is conjured into a statue "alive and ensouled." The witches, My Love, tell me that this bit of text finds its way into most Books of Shadows, so vital is it to our tradition. Yet I found this practiced, undimmed by time, in India and Tibet. The method that follows, drawn from the more complete Eastern practices, is easily applied by our fellows in the West.

Tantra, Dearest, recognizes an important factor in the psyche of the practitioner: intimacy with the God. The sundry strata of Yoga Tantra practices vary mostly in how close the aspirant feels to the Being invoked and the practices change their focus accordingly. Tantric Buddhism makes four distinct classes of this kind of practice: My Lord, My Friend, My Love, My Self.

As these distinctions can be but a matter of attitude (although they can also be ritualized), here at the beginning of such a path of development as I will lay out I will only make two distinctions, 'Generation in Front' which covers the first three classes, and 'Arising As'. Generation in Front is a means of approaching the God and cultivating a relationship with, in this case, 'Him'. Once cemented, the practitioner will learn to arise as the God Himself, eventually to wield His Power and Presence. While invoking 'in front' it will be up to you to determine the attitude you take to Ra-Hoor-Khuit. For you, is He Lord, Friend, or Lover?

This work is divided in 3 phases:

1. *Preliminary Practices*. These were mostly covered in the previous chapters but will be reviewed and developed here in explicitly Thelemic forms.
2. *Generation in Front*. We would call this evocation. This is when we invoke a Deity before us in order to receive blessings and to offer worship.
3. *The Post-transformation Practices*. Besides the Dedication of Merit, these are several practices that conclude the Work effectively. This concludes the first complete practice.

Once the basis has been acquired in the above practices, you can move on to the more intimate work:

A. *Arising As*. Building on the foundation of Generation in Front with a few modifications we then actually invoke and unite with the Deity.
B. *Fulfillment*. Having formed a connection with the deity through Generation in Front, and having developed that connection by Arising As, we next learn to wield the power of the Deity. This also includes elaborations on the basic Arising As practice.
C. *Initiation*. Having formed a union with the Deity we can then introduce others to the Deity, consecrating and empowering their ability to invoke the Deity.

Deep skill in Arising As and Fulfillment permits success in the advanced practices of *Yab-Yum*, or partner practice and *Ganachakra*, or group practice.

The ritual below (see ritual text in appendix, and find a PDF of it on the website: www.Concrescent.net) oscillates between recitation of verses from Liber AL and actual incantation and meditation. This forms a dramatic tension to propel the ritual and center the practice within the Thelemic mindstream. Having a copy of the full ritual alongside while reading this chapter will be helpful.

*The Preliminaries*

**Clearing—**

Rituals all begin with a way to separate the ritual time and place from ordinary time and location. Many begin with an act of purification. While this can be interpreted in many ways, in general it is to get rid of the unwanted and make present the desired influences. A practitioner of the Vajrayana would recite the 100-Syllable Vajrasattva (Diamond-being) Mantra. It is worth learning for this purpose, and for others, since it invokes the power of all the Buddhas at once. You should be able to find it on-line or in books, but it is traditional to acquire the oral transmission before using it. But a circle casting or banishing or whatever method you are comfortable with to set your space will work.

However, unless I or the space in which I am practicing is seriously disrupted I will generally dispense with the clearing activity and proceed to Refuge directly. I generally live in comity with the spirits about me, and as my allies,

I have no need of banishing them.

Once cleared of the unwanted it is time to invite those who will help. Beloved, let us remember, this is the essence of Refuge: we all need help. Refuge is asking for help, and then getting it. There are innumerable ways of doing this. Shortly we will apply one that uses sound and visualization along with sincere intention to conjure and receive that help—the Refuge by the 3 Ahs, which you have already learned and practiced.

But, to set this firmly on the path of Thelema, we will invoke the promise made us by the Lord of the Aeon Himself. We start with a slightly modified versicle (AL3.17) that summarizes the entire ritual before us as well as the immediate practice of refuge:

*Nu is my refuge as Hadit my light;*
*and Ra-Hoor-Khu is the strength, force, vigour, of my arms.*

It is sufficient by itself though we will reinforce it with the more energetic practice using the 3 Ahs once the spell that is this verse is spoken. In this rite we will continually draw out of the well of all forms, Nuit, the Ground of Being, inspired (enlightened/empowered) by the Divine incarnate in us as us, Hadit, and unite them into the Function and Force that is Ra-Hoor-Khu (-it). The verse taken from the Third Chapter, as you know, runs "and I am the strength...," as it is Ra-Hoor-Khuit speaking. His Name has been added to make the verse appropriate to someone as yourself who is using the verse as part of a practice. The 'Khu' form is chosen here to emphasize the presence of the Spirit of the Hawk-headed Lord more than one of His manifestations. We'll talk more about the 'Khu' in the section on Calling the Knowledge Being.

A particularly Thelemic way of Taking Refuge uses the stellar symbolism central to the Nuit chapter. As you sound the first 'A' the sun sets from the sky and the night stars come out. This is the "unveiling of the company of heaven" (AL1.2). If you can, imagine that you are floating in a field of stars with no earth below you. Each of the stars is one of the 'Company of Heaven,' one of those enlightened beings, or those who have vowed to aid, or the enlightened part of everyone around you. After all "Every man and every woman is a star" (AL1.3). As a whole, this image is of the Body of Nuit, Who is the Ground of Being.

On the second 'A' "the kisses of the stars rain hard upon thy body" (AL2.62). Each and every one of the stars lance a beam of light into your heart ("I am uplifted in thine heart," *ibid.*), skewering you, and igniting your being into a blazing white sphere, a star. Thus empowered you take your place in the Company of Stars.

As a star among stars you, and they, all sound the final 'A' and you behold Her light shed over all the Universe. Does She not say, "This shall regenerate the world, the little world my sister, my heart & my tongue, unto whom I send this kiss" (AL1.53)?

**Refuge—**
**Say:**
Nu is my refuge as Hadit my light;
and Ra-Hoor-Khu is the strength, force, vigour, of my arms.
**Sound:**
A—    *The unveiling of the company of heaven*
A—    *I am uplifted in thine heart;*
                    *and the kisses of the stars rain hard upon thy body.*
A—    *This shall regenerate the world, the little world my sister,*
                    *my heart & my tongue, unto whom I send this kiss.*

And so the drama has begun. We call upon our sources of refuge and arise empowered as a star in space. From this vantage point, with the second versicle the drama develops. This verse (AL2.9) distressed Crowley deeply since it seemed to contradict the Buddha's First Noble Truth "All is Sorrow". He was a victim of bad translation. The Buddha was speaking of the right motivation for entering into the Path: the recognition of the unsatisfactoriness of our experience. Only from awareness of this discomfort will we gain sufficient motivation to strive for enlightenment. However, from the Enlightened perspective which, of course, as the Tathagatagharba, the Buddha-Nature within all, Hadit would see from, All is Joyous, Pure and Present.

When we say this verse we are affirming the enlightened perspective and strive toward that state. Also, it affirms our soteriology, the 'salvation' that Thelema gives and the bodhisattvic-type commitment of the Thelemic Mage to make that salvation available to all. So we say the verse addressing the whole cosmos:

**Generating Bodhicitta—**
**Say:**
Remember all ye that existence is pure joy;
that all the sorrows are but as shadows;
they pass & are done; but there is that which remains.
*Imagine the verse shaking the cosmos, rattling those who are not awake enough to know its truth. They attend to your words rolling throughout the whole of being and reply in their hearts with a plaintive and useless 'why?' You, unshakable, simply model the reality with your adamantine commitment:*
**Say:**
All is pure and present, and has always been so.
To this realization I commit myself:
Pure and Total presence.

Is this not the same as "Let there be no difference made among you between any one thing & any other thing; for thereby there cometh hurt" (AL1.22)? Say this three to five times and then pause to let it sink in. Let go of your thoughts and just show up into the present moment and place.

To sharpen our Bodhicitta still further and to deepen our dedication to the this specific invocation and its result we formulate our intention in a vow. This vow binds our work to its ultimate purpose and reciprocally binds the thrust of the Cosmos, which is in the direction of enlightenment, to our efforts.

**Dedication Vow—**
**Say:**
I hereby dedicate my practice
of this Invocation of Ra-Hoor-Khuit
to the benefit of all beings, including myself,
and upon attaining to the realization that it gives,
I dedicate that power to aid all beings
to the supreme realization called Enlightenment.

It is vital that we gather up and apply all of the resources we can bring to bear in an invocation like this. We must not neglect Those who brought us to these ways and Those who have gone before us. Let us remember that we are at the leading edge of a wavefront that stretches back through time. By invoking it we both continue Their work and acquire Their aid.

**Invoking Lineage—**
**Say:**
I invoke those who have gone before me
I invoke the Shamans, the Magi and the Witches
Who founded my practices
I invoke the Orders that preserved and transmitted the Way
I invoke the Teachers who taught me the Way
Bless me, sustain me, empower me in my practice
For I am one of you, true heir and descendent
In me the Way lives, aid me!

So far, Dearest, you have learned two forms of empowerment and union with the Teacher. Here is a specific form for this practice drawn from a careful reading of our Holy Text. It applies the means you have already learned but the embodiment of the Teacher is now the Goddess Ra-Hoor-Khut (see AL3.1). Throughout the Text there are several variations on the spelling of the Name. In ancient Egyptian, the '-t' ending indicates the feminine, so Ra-Hoor-Khu with the 't', Ra-Hoor-Khut, is a Goddess.

The Witches often say all Goddesses are one Goddess and all Gods are one God. To understand Ra-Hoor-Khut, similar thoughts apply. In Thelema, if we were to unite the Deities this way, all Deities resume themselves in Nuit and Hadit. Classical Neoplatonism shows us that ultimate powers create instances of themselves at each level of being suitable to that domain. The level here is empowerment.

Nuit is abstract and, even understood as the night sky, difficult to connect with as an embodiment. To deliver her empowerment in such an anthropomorphic context as we are working here, She presents Herself in the form of Ra-Hoor-Khut. Indeed, My Love, this is no different than Hadit presenting himself as Ra-Hoor-Khuit.

To do this we use the first verses of each of the Three Chapters, a profound and powerful incantation to conjure Her. These verses recapitulate the process of Creation in a Thelemic mode.

**Empowerment by Ra-Hoor-Khut—**

| **Say:** | **See:** |
|---|---|
| Had! | *Sound,* |
| The manifestation | *and a golden Winged Globe* |
| of Nuit. | *appears before you* |
| | |
| Nu! | *Sound, and the Globe folds its wings* |
| the hiding of Hadit. | *and is wrapped in darkness like the night sky, hidden* |
| | |
| Abrahadabra; | *Sound, and the darkness is riven by lightning* |
| the reward of | *The Lightning Flash forms into Ra-Hoor-Khut,* |
| Ra Hoor Khut. | *with flesh of lapis lazuli, hair of jet,* |
| | *red Egyptian garb with gold ornaments.* |

As you sound the syllable 'Had' (of which we will get much more use to come), visualize a sphere of metallic gold before you, perhaps with fluttering wings. It is flashing gold light in all directions, illuminating the world, and gathering that light back into itself making it ever more golden. This is the egg in which the Godform from which you will take empowerment will arise. It is a manifestation of the Ground of Being Itself called before you by this mighty spell.

As you sound 'Nu!' the 'egg' is wrapped in the night-womb of space to incubate it. Whereas before it radiated light and gathered it up, it now takes the resources so collected and in the isolation of its own autonomy assembles them into the form it shall become.

As you sound the Word of the Lightning Flash, 'Abrahadabra', let the Night be split by lightning from which steps Ra-Hoor-Khut with skin the flame-blue of lapis lazuli, Her hair jet-black, and wearing red Egyptian dress with gold jewelry. But then, some see her Hawk-headed with the sky-blue nemmes.

Note that the Lightning Flash still plays within Her form for She dwells ever at the moment of creation. She comes and stands before you. Then, as you sound the following syllables they arise brilliant as stars on Her body.

**Adorning with Syllables—**
**Sound:**

HAD— *On the Brow of Ra-Hoor-Khut appears a White Winged Globe*
RE— *At the Throat of Ra-Hoor-Khut appears a Red Solar Disk*
NU— *At the Heart of Ra-Hoor-Khut appears a Blue Nu Pot*
AL— *At the Navel of Ra-Hoor-Khut appears a Golden Aleph-Lamed*

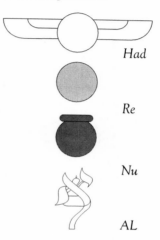

Had

Re

Nu

AL

The Globe is white for the purity and health of the Body, the Solar Disk is red for the energy of Speech, the Nu Pot is blue for the sky-like spaciousness of the Mind, and the AL is gold for the incorruptible Will.

Now pray in all fervency as did the Scribe in Cairo those many long years ago, and She will answer you. While your prayer, My Love, is to Nuit, it is delivered through Ra-Hoor-Khut for the power of this rite is formed in body, and Nuit ultimately lies beyond form and embodiment.

**Receiving Empowerment—**
**Say:**

Who am I and what shall be the sign? So she answered him, bending down, a lambent flame of blue, all touching, all penetrant, her lovely hands upon the black earth, & her lithe body arched for love, and her soft feet not hurting the little flowers: Thou knowest! And the sign shall be my ecstasy, the consciousness of the continuity of existence, the omnipresence of my body [the unfragmentary non-atomic fact of my universality].

**Sound:**

HAD— *Reach out to the White Winged Globe on the Brow of Ra-Hoor-Khut with both of your hands. Lift it off Her Brow (where it yet remains) and draw it to your own, trailing light back to Hers. Place it on your brow and feel the purification of your flesh pour throughout your body.*

RE— *Reach out to the Red Solar Disk at the Throat of Ra-Hoor-Khut and draw it to your throat, whereupon appears a Red Solar Disk empowering your speech and energy.*

NU— *And again with the Blue Nu Pot at the Heart of Ra-Hoor-Khut, to your heart, whereon appears a Blue Nu Pot empowering your mind.*

AL— *Finally from the Golden AL at the Navel of Ra-Hoor-Khut draw to your navel, whereon appears a Golden AL empowering your will.*

A— *(Ah) Sound, and Ra-Hoor-Khut and all realized beings sound with you. Ra-Hoor-Khut dissolves from back to front until only the syllables remain which then travel up the beams of light and unite with the syllables on you, granting all empowerments and becoming of one taste with you. Rest.*

*The Two Accumulations*

Remember, My Dear, two accumulations follow empowerment and serve to collect your personal resources to strengthen your invocation. As experience shows, much of the spiritual path is a matter of collecting enough energy to make whatever it is you are looking for happen. This cultivation of power is done both directly through will and indirectly through practices of compassion and wisdom. The universal will is towards the ever-increasing and non-climaxing intensity and harmony of feeling, which we experience subjectively as the drive to be happy and objectively as the desire to improve (optimize) our circumstance. When we act to support this drive, which the Buddhists call the 'Buddha-nature' or 'Tathagatagarbha', the universe supports us with a gift of power. Wielding this power requires focusing it. This is what we will be doing through the act of Deity Yoga itself. However, to be able to focus the universal power, which itself is an act of form, requires that we master the universal form, which is formlessness. This, the Buddhists term wisdom.

The first accumulation, as you know, is called 'the Four Immeasurables' and gathers your good karma through an act of well-wishing. By blessing others for their benefit it gives you practice in generosity and creates a flow of your good karma, called your 'merit', and puts you in the midst of that stream. This is an act of Bodhicitta that, since you are doing the will of the Universe, gives you the resources of the Universe to draw on. This is part of that essential Mahayanist insight that the Supreme Enlightenment is only available to those who can harness the drive power of the universe through embodying the compassion of divine providence. But Thelemically, and in accord with the drama of the rite and the character of the Deity, we take a wrathful view to compassion.

This is one of the elements of Thelema that gets it in trouble. A prime example of this is the verse (below) which we will use to open this section. Fear not, My Love, Tantra comes to the rescue. Tantra is all about not ignoring or suppressing our emotions and passions, but harnessing them to the task of liberation and enlightenment. Naturally, anger is not ignored, but turned to the task and purified in the process. For it is right, meet, and proper that we wage continuous war against suffering, and actions against this true foe can be fiery, and this fire is compassion. In Tantric Buddhism, there are (roughly) three classes of Buddhas and Bodhisattvas: Peaceful, Joyous and Wrathful, and the Wrathful Buddhas are seen as the most compassionate ones. This is because they are specifically active to transform the situation from worse to better. They, in one form or another, wield the cosmic clue-by-four of enlightenment, and tend to deliver it upon our heads when we are being stupid. (The appropriate response is "Thank you, Master.") They come in forms with fangs and flames, swords and skull-bowls brimming with blood, roaring with laughter and rage at stupidity and suffering. In traditional iconography they trample under their feet the specific foes they destroy, such as attachment and aversion, unenlightened passion and wrath, fear and stupidity. This may seem odd, but the Wrathful ones are not as terrifying as the Peaceful ones.

Their calm, to beings like us, is far more frightening than a vast being bearing down on us with a sword. Thus is Ra-Hoor-Khuit a wrathful form but only a mild one. Compare Him with Vajrakilaya and He looks gentle.

Thelema is a religion of Kings, or Sovereigns if you prefer, Dear Lady. Counseled by Hadit to "veil not your vices in virtuous words" etc. (AL2.52), 'vice' here in our spoken verse has a subtle meaning, easily misunderstood. If we take compassion as mere niceness, it is a vice is the usual sense, but if we take up our duty to end the sickness of the world it becomes a vice as Hadit means it in verse 52, an action of wrath in which we delight (AL3.46) that does destruction to the wretch and weakling.

*My Husband, how can this be?*

If you would destroy the thirsty, give them to drink! If you would destroy the hungry, give them to eat! Fools falling into the pit called Because (AL2.27) will use this verse to justify the horror of violence and abuse. This is a trap for those unworthy of Thelema. But you, knowing the Truth of the Gods, know They are wholly good and They do not incite us to evil.

So, stamp down upon the wretched and the weak by liberating them from their suffering, and delight in it! Here, we do so with the power of magick. We declare our conviction with the verse and then wield the power of the Four Immeasurables to end misery and protect the vulnerable. As we have discussed this in depth earlier I give only the summary direction of the practice here.

**The Four Immeasurables—**
**Say:**
Compassion is the vice of kings: stamp down the wretched & the weak: this is the law of the strong: this is our law and the joy of the world. (AL2.21)
**Sound (4, 16, or 20x):**
A—  *Awaken Loving Kindness–Compassion–Joy in their Joy–Equanimity*
      *Toward:*
      *Yourself–All who are close to you–All who are connected to you–*
      *All who you know of–To the non-objectified All*

Before the power conjured by the compassionate practice of the Four Immeasurables can be used, the capacity to direct or focus this power must be cultivated through a practice of wisdom. What the Buddhists and the Thelemites discovered is that the origin of form comes from the formless. Thus to master form, one must cultivate the awareness of and intimacy with the formless, the mother of all form.

To get there we use the versicle that shows us the union of our individual will with the primal void, not as some theoretical construct, My Dear, but as a profound injunction which some magi take as their obligation upon initiation.

One can understand this verse (see practice below) as follows, My Love, although it is whole unto itself as an incantation. Having gathered up your meritorious karma, which can be said to be your only true possession: your past actions and their result, this 'all' is to be thrown into the work. The work is to do your will, which as Thelemites we know is inalienably rooted in the Divine Will, and by doing that there is nothing that can oppose us such that even in failing we succeed. When we have refined ourselves until we are only operating out of our Divine Legacy our will is pure. Being rooted in the Divine it is invariant, however dynamic and complex. Being freed from attachment to the outcome of our action, part of the refining process, every vector of effect is in keeping with Divine Intent and thus perfect.

But suddenly with this verse we leap from the personal to the ontological. That in perfection, meaning complete and wholly itself, each perfect thing or act is united in the Grand Unity of Being, which while 'one' in its character, is better seen as 'none', namely that Void-Ground out of which all comes. Insightful as is this as a revelation, as a spell the properly prepared practitioner can use the seed-syllable 'None' to enter into the Void dissolving all as the sound fades into silence. I'll remind you that the 'Nun' in ancient Egypt is the formless ocean out of which arises the Primal Mound, and the first God, Atum (Atom).

Thus, it is possible that the verse alone would be enough, but rarely are we so skilled and practiced that with that final word can we enter wholly into the None. If you have, enjoy it, and in due time you will find yourself in the midst of the invocation of the Deity. But mostly we need this extra, albeit simple, practice:

### Entering the Ground of Being—
**Say:**
So with thy all; thou hast no right but to do thy will.
Do that, and no other shall say nay.
For pure will, unassuaged of purpose,
delivered from the lust of result, is every way perfect.
The Perfect and the Perfect are one Perfect and not two;
nay, are none!
**Sound:**
Nun— *and you take on the godform of Nun or Nuit, i.e., anthropomorphic with a Nu-pot (see Syllables of Adornment) on your head, while you observe the universe of Form dissolving into the Formless Ocean of Nun.*
**Sound:**
Nun— *and Your Body dissolves slowly from below into the Formless Ocean, leaving only the spherical Nu-pot.*
**Sound:**
Nun— *and Nu-pot slowly dissolves from the bottom, through its girth, to its mouth which dissolves off into the Void-Ocean of the Nun like the sound of a singing bowl. Rest—*

End your sound as the rim of the Nu-pot vanishes and let your mind, all of your thoughts and attentions dissolve off into Shunyata, the primal formless ocean of being. A Nu-pot is a spherical hollow vessel with a rim and used for holding or boiling water, usually kept upright on a stand. Inverted it is the bowl of the sky, and thus Nut or Nuit. Completed with the wavy n-glyph representing water it is Nun, the name of the primordial ocean and the God who is its embodiment.

Rest there in the natural state of the mind, neither provoking thoughts nor chasing after those that arise. Cultivate this as long as you can. It is from here that you will launch into the Deity Yoga itself, My Love.

*Then let us rest here a moment, My Priest...*

# 7
# Generation in Front

Beloved, now that you have practiced the preliminaries such that you can draw upon the resources available to you, fortified yourself with them, cultivated the right attitude, gathered your karma like stored momentum, and, through knowing the secret union of form and emptiness, dissolved the Universe into Its state before creation, you are now ready to begin the principal work.

The first task is to learn to invoke the Ra-Hoor-Khuit before you, or 'In Front' as the Tantrics call it. (Technically, we of the West call this 'evocation' since it happens 'outside' of you.) In this form you will cultivate your relationship to the Deity. Once sufficient intimacy has been developed, you will be ready to 'arise as' the Deity. Then you will be able to wield the powers of the Deity as your own. Until then you can request the blessing of those powers for yourself and others. Later, after you have mastered both of these skills, you will practice doing both at once and then be able to transmit this practice to others by the rite of Empowerment.

Darling, the essence of what we are doing is recapitulating Creation and Birth. Having returned all to the Void we then begin to remake the World in the image of the Deity.

The process of invoking a Deity 'In Front' has 7 stages:
1. Forming the Deity Image
2. Adorning the Deity with Syllables or Symbols
3. Calling the 'Knowledge Being' or Spirit of the Deity
4. Initiating this new incarnation of the Deity
5. Welcoming, Offering and Praise
6. Arousing the Heart and Receiving Blessing
7. Radiating Forth and Gathering In.

This method is the same technique, at least in general outlines if not in specifics, used in the Hermetic text called the Asclepius wherein the spirit of a being was called down to inhabit a statue. For our work the Deity can be invoked into a statue or any other suitable object, or simply into a visualization. Nonetheless, all we are doing is creating an embodiment for the Deity, imaginal or physical, providing it with the means to articulate Itself, then inviting an emanation of the Deity to inhabit the embodiment and bring it to life, and finally to seal the spirit of the Deity into the embodiment and bless it. After this we simply treat the embodiment as the Deity. Contrary to the polemics against idolatry, we no more confuse the statue or visualization with the Deity than we confuse a telephone with the person we are talking to.

We left off the last action sitting in the void, Shunyata, immersed in the sheer spaciousness of the Ground of Being. In here and from here all things arise, including Ra-Hoor-Khuit. One should remain in this state, absorbed in Shunyata as long as possible, cultivating the state, until the drive to give rise to the Deity becomes overwhelming. The feeling should be one of physical and spiritual compulsion.

United with the Not, My Love, and as Her agent, a star in the Body of Nuit, we are compelled by our compassion and wisdom to answer the challenge of existence. It is as though, in the Void, we still hear the cries of sentient beings suffering and must respond. We do this by giving birth to the being who is the Solution.

When this compulsion becomes too great to resist, we sound the seed syllable of the Deity. This is easy in Vajrayana practice since all beings have an affiliation with one of the Buddha families, and each family has its own seed syllable. This has very broad practical implications. Chiefly, you always know the root of the Deity you are working with. Also, when a text like a tantra is associated with a Deity, it may provide a seed syllable. But when a text is not available, research or contemplation can provide a syllable for Deities not already possessing one. Syllables, glyphs, sigils and pantacles visualized will aid while pronouncing the Deity's name.

We, Love, are working with a contemporary recension of an Egyptian Deity, one it can be argued not actually found in the ancient texts, so they may be of little help. We have the fortune of Frater Achad's insight into our source text the Book of the Law. From this we take the full Latin title of our scripture, Liber AL vel Legis. Here we find the Hebrew particle Aleph Lamed,

which serves as a key to the text and means 'God'. In the ancient Canaanite culture from which the Hebrew Israelite tradition comes, 'Al' is the name of the father of the Gods, roughly equivalent to Cronos or Saturn in the Olympian pantheon. With this venerable pedigree we will take AL as our seed syllable (see illustrations). To bring this together into a unitary form, and for beauty's sake, we will create a monogram of it and make the glyph in yellow, properly metallic gold, below.

There is an irony in using this syllable for an Egyptian God. The Egyptians did not have a letter 'L', conflating the liquid phoneme with 'R' as do the Chinese. If you will indulge me in a bit of Hieroglyphic Qabalah or letter analysis, the Egyptians would write 'Aleph Lamed' with the 'Vulture' over the 'Mouth'. Clearly the mouth can mean speech, but the vulture is a silent bird and so used for the glottal stop as is the Aleph in Hebrew. Further the vulture is Mut, the Mother. And so this glyph combination can be read as the silent Mother given voice, or the Void speaking.

As before we will begin this section with another verse from the Book of the Law. Liber AL gives us a marvelous set of verses that describe, embody and evoke this process. In it the Scribe, enfolded in the embrace of the Not, receiving Her empowerment, longs for complete dissolution into the Void. Yet that Void is creative and compassionate. She corrects the scribe in his desire to retreat from the challenge of manifestation. She gives us then the words of creation, perhaps the most important spell in the Book. She tells us how and why 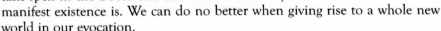 manifest existence is. We can do no better when giving rise to a whole new world in our evocation.

While still immersed in the formlessness of Shunyata we begin the play of form and drama cultivating with the verse of the empowerment by Nuit. Feeling that empowerment and the emotions that spontaneously arise with it we begin the process of separation from the homogeneous Void of the Nun by addressing Her with our desire to remain ever in union. On a practical basis, when entering into the void, after a time we find dualistic and conceptual awareness returning. As this happens, we needn't say them but rather recollect and identify with the words of the Scribe as modeled in our scripture:

**Conjuring the Godform—**
**Perceiving silently:**
Then the priest answered & said unto the Queen of Space, kissing her
lovely brows, and the dew of her light bathing his whole body in a sweet-
smelling perfume of sweat:

*Out of the heartache of separating from the Whole of Being pray fervently as did*
*the Scribe—*
**Say:**
O Nuit, continuous one of Heaven, let it be ever thus;
that men speak not of Thee as One but as None;
and let them speak not of thee at all,
since thou art continuous!

*Then imagine your whisper as her voice in response. . .*
**Say (whisper):**
None, breathed the light, faint & faery, of the stars, and two.
For I am divided for love's sake, for the chance of union.
This is the creation of the world, that the pain of division is as nothing, and
the joy of dissolution all.

The wise will recognize that final 'all' as none other than 'AL' and it can
be the first sounding of the generative seed syllable. It gives an important
indication of the work.

With the **first sounding** the syllable itself arises alone in and from the
Void, self-luminous and metallic Gold. Is not Ra-Hoor-Khuit a Solar God?
Since we are generating 'in front' see the AL hanging in space before you.

As there is nothing else in existence, the syllable itself **sounds its name
again** and golden, honeyed light radiates from the syllable throughout all
Space and returns on the inhale gathering up the power of the Deity invoked
into the syllable transforming it into a Golden Sphere or Egg. A Deity, who
is the embodiment of some power or principle of the Universe, is herewith
created by and as a manifestation of that power. With this God, My Love, I
see Ra-Hoor-Khuit as the embodiment of the union of the Wills of the Enlightened Ones.

Lastly, **sound AL a third time** and this time the light goes out from the
syllable blessing all beings throughout space, fulfilling their wills and dissolving the Golden Sphere, draining it from the top down like a lake leaving in
its midst the form of Ra-Hoor-Khuit enthroned on a Rose. Envision Him as
if you are Ankh-af-na-khonsu facing Him in the Stele of Revealing or as the
Æon Trump in the Thoth Tarot deck. You can use the card as your icon. Al-
ternatively, you can use the icon of Ra-Hoor-Khuit developed for this practice
and adorning the cover of the book. It is available for download from the
website.

To strengthen our connection and to affirm His nature, we salute the God
before us with His revelation verse.

**Saluting the God—**
**Say:**
Ra-Hoor-Khuit hath taken his seat in the East at the Equinox of the Gods...
Hoor in his secret name and splendour is the Lord initiating.

In order to give the Deity ways of interacting with us and His environment,
we adorn Ra-Hoor-Khuit with syllables at the chakra centers. This is exactly
the same as we did in the empowerment phase above. In general we can use
just three syllables for body, speech and mind, or there can be more for each
of the other chakras and even more can be added all over the Deity's body if
desired. The purpose is to provide means of articulation for the activities of
the Deity—interfaces, so to speak, into different areas of activity. Since will is
so central to Thelemic practice we include 'AL' at the navel to articulate the
God's will.

This is done by sounding the syllables and visualizing them arising at the
corresponding points of the Deity's body. To start, we bless the process with
two verses:

**Adorning with Syllables—**
**Say:**
Burn upon their brows, o splendrous serpent!
O azure-lidded woman, bend upon them!
**Sound (all in one breath):**
HAD—RE—NU—AL *and a white winged globe appears on the brow of Ra-Hoor-*
*Khu-it, a red solar disk appears at His throat, a blue Nu pot appears at His heart,*
*with an "A" inside it, and a gold AL appears at His navel.*
**With the next breath sound:**
A— *(Ah) from the small 'A' in the Nu pot, and all is suffused with bliss, and the*
*Gate of the Duat opens before you.*

*Calling the Khu*
    What we have so far is a visualization with interfaces into the world. Now
we have to get the Deity itself to show up. Praise to get the attention of the
Deity and prayer to ask the Deity to come works here, but it must be backed
up with sincerity and single-pointed focus.
    As you sound the final 'Ah' above, imagine a gateway to the Duat, the
stainless Abode of the Gods, before and above you. I see it made of wrought
iron between two pillars. Centered on the gate and splitting apart when it
opens is a five-pointed star with a red circle in the middle.
    As the 'Ah' trails off or as the adoration proceeds the Gate opens and a
Hawk crowned with the Sun lands on the lintel as a perch to listen to your
praises. The Hawk is a presentation of the essence of the Deity, the embodiment of His intelligence or consciousness. This is one of the Egyptian seven
'souls' and is called by the Golden Dawn the 'Khu.' (Scholars today generally

use 'Akh'.) It will animate the image you have created and be the part of the actual God present in the visualization or icon.

Dear One, we have two major incantations with which to call the Khu of Ra-Hoor-Khuit. They are the "Aka Dua" chant from the Stele of Revealing, or the paraphrase of the Adoration composed by Crowley from the translation of the Stele, of which the 'Aka Dua' is the second verse (see below). Either will work alone but on a practical basis, I often use them both.

*The Aka Dua chant*
Aka dua / tuf ur biu / bia che fu / dudu nur af / an nuteru

When I use the Adoration of Ankh-af-na-khonsu, found first on the Stele of Revealing and paraphrased in the Book of the Law, I vary it because I am not Ankh-af-na-khonsu and his name is written into its fabric. Further I am neither a Theban nor a prophet (forth-speaker) of Mentu. But, I am of Earth and a Mage who works for Horus. Self-slain is a claim made by Egyptian priests referring to their initiation, but I often use self-made as below. Lastly, in proper Egyptian mode Ankh-af-na-khonsu mentions his mother and father, which I do not share. I find Therion and Babalon suitable replacements. Do this as you will. The important point is to be sincere and passionate.

**Calling the Knowledge Being—**
**Say or Sing:**
I am a Lord of Earth, and I
    The inspired forth-speaker of Heru;
For me unveils the veiléd sky,
    The self-made *use own name*
Whose words are truth. I invoke, I greet
    Thy presence, O Ra-Hoor-Khuit!

Unity uttermost showed!
    I adore the might of Thy breath,
Supreme and terrible God,
    Who makest the gods and death
To tremble before Thee:—
    I, I adore thee!

Appear on the throne of Ra!
    Open the ways of the Khu!
Lighten the ways of the Ka!
    The ways of the Khabs run through
To stir me or still me!
    Aum! let it fill me!

The light is mine; its rays consume
 Me: I have made a secret door
Into the house of Ra and Tum,
 Of Khephra and of Ahathoor.
I am Mage, O Heru,
 The prophet *use own name*!

By Therion my breast I beat;
 By Babalon I weave my spell.
Show thy star-splendour, O Nuit!
 Bid me within thine House to dwell,
O wingéd snake of light, Hadit!
Abide with me, Ra-Hoor-Khuit!

A visualization accompanies the adoration for the verse starting with "Appear on the throne of Ra!" With the first line the Khu leaves the Gate, stoops through the top of the godform's head, and alights on the AL syllable at the navel. The Heart-Mind of the godform is filled with the Divine Presence at 'Khu.' The Energy-Speech is filled with the Divine Presence at 'Ka.' The Body is filled with the Divine Presence with 'Khabs.' And finally all is filled with bliss with 'Aum.'

I perform a few gestures while saying this adoration. I point to the quarters when listing the Solar Deities (see Initiation below). I strike my breast with my left hand, not in penance but in salute and affirmation at 'Therion,' and raise my right fist, arm square (see Anubis kneeling) I lower and sweep them as though spreading a fabric at 'Babalon,' like the High Priestess Trump in the Thoth Deck. Finally, like in Liber V vel Reguli, I draw a circle overhead at 'Nuit,' touch my Base chakra at 'Hadit' and my Heart at 'Ra-Hoor-Khuit,' using the thumb between fore and middle fingers gesture.

At times I replace the second verse with the Aka Dua, or just mix it in repeating the English verse before and/or after the Egyptian. I usually sing this adoration to a melody recorded by a New York band called the Heretics in the 1980s.

Once the spirit of the Deity takes its place in the Deity-form, seal the spirit into the form and make it firm by uniting it to the created form through incantation. The Vajrayana use "Jah-Hum-Bam-Hoh." I will leave it to you to find a suitable interpretation. As a Thelemite I simply use "Abrahadabra," meaning most appropriately here, 'it is created as it is spoken.'

**Sealing in the Spirit—**
**Sound:**
Abrahadabra! (3x)

One special quality of Abrahadabra, which can be called the Word of Manifestation or Action, is that having eleven letters, as it is sounded it recapitulates the Lightning Flash on the Tree of Life, one letter to each Sephira including Daath. So, as you sound this Word to seal in the Khu, see each letter of it lighting up in the corresponding location on the body of Ra-Hoor-Khuit and the brilliance of the Lightning Flash they trace. (This distorts the pronunciation in interesting ways, drawing out each letter as you descend the Tree.) It is through this that the function is accomplished and the Spirit of the God is sealed into the 'Flesh' you have created.

Abrahadabra also has a seven-fold and a five-fold pronunciation. The seven-fold is pronounced as "A.ba.ra.ha.da.ba.ra" and can be associated with the scale of the planets. The five-fold is pronounced "Ab.ra.had.ab.ra" and can be associated with the scale of the elements. The seven-fold is particularly good for repetitive chanting and the five- for declaiming. When sealing in the spirit, use all three pronunciations. The eleven-fold is able to establish the Lightning Flash and invoke the Sephiroth, the seven-fold to invoke the planets, and the five-fold to invoke the elements, recreating and articulating the three main strata of being.

The last stage in making the Deity present is initiation. This is done to inaugurate this incarnation of the Deity, (further) seal it into its body, and fully invest it with all power and authority. The method is a visualization of the ancient rite of anointing which was done to kings at their coronation. Here instead of holy oil, the Deity is anointed with Divine light-nectar. Those who are doing the anointing are, for the Buddhists, the heads of the five Buddha families. These are the 'Tathagatas', the 'thus-going ones.' For Thelemites like ourselves, My Dear, we have just invoked the four faces of the Sun as it goes through the day. Requiring a fifth, to this we will add Heru-ra-ha to complete the set. As we have just called them in the preceding adoration we do not also say a verse here. Please note, My Love, that we use the Egyptian arraignment here and not that of the Golden Dawn. Khephra is to the ancient ones the dawn, not midnight, and with Ra as noon, and Atum as the setting, the House of Horus, Het-Hoor, can only be midnight. We begin with a Summons:

### Initiation by the Solar Gods—
**Say:**
From the Abodes of Life, I conjure the Sun!
**Sound:**
A—   (Ah) *Call for aid from all Realized Beings, the Ground of Being Itself and the Potential for Enlightenment in all Beings. These arrive in the form of the Solar Gods: Khephra, the Beetle in the East; Ra, the Hawk-headed Man in the South; Atum the Man in the West; Het-Hoor, the Woman with Cow-horns and Solar Disk in the North; Heru-ra-ha in the form of the Winged Disk in the Center*

*(above). They each bear a crystal flask filled with glowing white nectar formed from innumerable white letter 'A's, and array Themselves about Ra-Hoor-Khuit.*

**Sound:**

A— *They pour their blessing nectar onto and through the top of His head, filling Him like a flask to overflowing. The overflow becomes the Solar Disk on His head with the Uraeus Serpent erect within it.*

**Sound:**

A— *The God now initiated, the Solar Gods dissolve and pour themselves into the God, becoming 'of one taste' with Him and the image of which becomes alive and sparkling.*

### Greetings, Offerings, & Praise

At this point, My Dear, we have done the work of getting the Deity before us, but now our relationship with the Deity determines what we are to do. In the various flavors of Yoga Tantra, namely Action (Karma), Performance (Kriya), and Yoga Tantra itself, one of the main distinguishing factors is how intimate we are with the Deity. Think of how differently you would behave if meeting the President of the United States or the Queen of England, versus meeting a friend, versus meeting a lover! Who would you bow to, shake hands with, or embrace and kiss? We engage in ritual actions called decorum that match the degree of closeness we feel. Practically, we may use all of them in ritual. At first we may prostrate ourselves, then be the solicitous host, then be the cozy intimate.

So, My Love, how do you feel about Ra-Hoor-Khuit? With the God before you, will you prostrate yourself? Some cry 'bend not the knee', but in ritual we use social artifice to accomplish our purpose, without ever being subordinate, or rather no more subordinate than any human is before a God. Remember, the *Gnothi Seauton*, oft translated 'Know Thyself' really means "[Human,] Know Thy Place." In our right place we have enormous influence; being wrong here is hubris, and dangerous. Bowing or kneeling in any form is an act of submission, true, but here it functions as a 'yin' activity, an anode to the Divine cathode, and initiates a flow from the God to yourself. It beats upon our narrow egos and makes them more sensitive to the Deity's signal and capable of receiving His blessing. Choose wisely.

As a whole, this kind of evocation is in the social mode of "welcoming the honored guest". In the same way as we welcome a guest at the door, take their coat, tell them how glad we are to see them, sit them down and offer them refreshment, we do the same for our divine guest.

Your work thus far has brought Him in the door and seated Him. At this point you directly address Ra-Hoor-Khuit before you. It is good to place physical food and other offerings on the altar. Experience shows that the quality of the materials and the sincerity of the offering have great impact. Yet to a certain level, it also seems that by giving mass to the Deities They are more present in the physical realm. The more physical the desired outcome of the rite, the more important it is that the offering be physical. But not necessary.

For you may use visualizations to make the offerings and, like the physical ones, see the Deity accepting them. With imaginal offerings you have the special advantage that you can make them expand to as vast a quantity as you can conceive and make them to be "exactly as You like them" in your prayers. Much of the time it is worth doing both.

While the God is enjoying refreshment, offer praise. Songs, poems or words from the heart create a strong connection between the speaker and the hearer and 'dispose' the Deity to being of help.

In traditional Yoga Tantra there is in some cases a mantra or special prayer of the Deity recited for a time to 'arouse the heart' of the Deity, which is a euphemism for motivating the Deity to act on your behalf. We will do this after refreshing and strengthening the visualization.

### Greetings—
*Welcome Ra-Hoor-Khuit in whatever manner seems best to you.*

Now, offer refreshment and gifts. We begin this part with a slight tweak on verse AL3.34, which should be self-explanatory, and continue with a crib from tantric offering technique, translated into a Thelemic mode and English.

### Offerings—
**Say:**
May blessing now be poured To the Hawk-headed mystical Lord!
**Say or Sing:**
Had!—Re!—Nu!— Abrahadabra!
Ra-Hoor-Khu-it: To you and all your host we offer,
Form, Sound, Smell, Taste, and Touch, the Whole of Space,
Father's Milk and Mother's Blood, [and] the Fruit of Existence
Come and Enjoy!

The first line fires up our chakras and the three dimensions of our existence, Brow/Body, Throat/Speech-Energy, Heart/Mind, and then we use the Word of Manifestation to empower what we are about to bring forth. The next lines address the offering to the recipient, and for good measure we include any others of His host or retinue who may be accompanying Him. In this simplest version of the rite, only Ra-Hoor-Khuit is present. This can be elaborated on to include Nuit, Hadit, Therion, Babalon, and others, and can be expanded infinitely.

The next line offers the five senses. Understand that each word refers to and offers the object of the sense, the means of sensation and the act of sensing, but as that would be too long-winded to say, we use one word as a reference to each. In the older traditions there is an understanding of the mind itself as the sixth sense. We use the image of the vastness of Space to offer this.

Next we offer the two bases of existence, the Father and Mother principals, semen poetically called milk and the female equivalent as blood, although we, and the Tantrics, know that menstrual blood is not fertile. Finally, we offer an emblem of all good things, expressed as the Fruit of Existence, to include everything in the world not covered above. And, naturally, at the end we say, *Bon Appétit!*

*My Husband, I had a dream the other night that taught me of this offering way.*

Please, My Love, My Wife, tell it to me.

*I was a Spirit on the other side of the Veil, in training to become one of those who helps the incarnate to pass between the worlds, and to work with them in mediating all things of magic and spirit. I myself have a teacher in this world, who was taking me for the first time to the boundary with the world of matter. As we descended, I felt an uncomfortable pressure building up, and it became harder and harder to continue downward, and was forced to flee upward again. My teacher told me not to worry, because those whom we were on our way to visit knew what they were doing and would make the way easier. He gave me something in the way of assistance that allowed me to continue descending.*

*As we approached the boundary, I became more aware of these incarnate beings whom we were visiting. The pressure or density was very great, but my teacher showed me to the Offering that had been dedicated to me, a plate of candy canes. He showed me how to take within myself some of the essence of the food and drink they had laid out. As I did so the pressure lessened tremendously and I was able to stay in this place much more easily. He then taught me more concerning the energies that were being worked within this Circle. As I sucked on the candy cane, I expressed concern that the content of the Offering would be used up too soon. The trainer told me it was okay, the people who had invoked us to visit were well trained in how to titrate how much offering was needed to keep us able to play in their world, and they would not call us only to leave us hungry. After a time I began to feel the pressure of dense matter building up again, and I absorbed more of the essence of the Offerings and was comfortably able to continue longer. In this way I was able to take my practical training in this place at the Veil between the Worlds until the Circle was done and it was time to return.*

I cannot add to this.

From the social connection with the Greeting, to the material connection with the Offering, we now turn to connection at the level of speech, energy and emotion with the Praise. The very best way is extemporaneous. The spontaneity keeps us at the crest of the wave front of the present. The mind is wholly caught up in the process and single pointed. Even more powerfully, the feedback of the immediate experience guides the words to bring us as close as we can manage to the God. It has the further virtue of not conditioning us to the practice such that our minds slip over the words without really reaping the benefit of their effect.

Nonetheless, others' beautiful and meaningful words can transport us. The first invocation of Ra-Hoor-Khuit, although not yet known by that name, and performed by Crowley in Cairo at the vernal Equinox before receiving the Book of the Law in 1904, has special power. Written, or perhaps more aptly termed designed by his wife, Rose Kelly Crowley, and composed by Crowley, it has been noted that due to its trans-cultural structure, it may have been the first modern Pagan invocation. Properly called the "Invocation of Horus according to the vision of Ouarda the Seer." It is available on the website for your use.

I have composed another (briefer) example by cribbing lines from both the Book of the Law and from Liber Tzaddi, presented below.

**Praise—**
**Say:**
Thou! the Hawk-headed Lord of Silence and of Strength,
    Thy nemmes shrouds the night blue sky
Thou! Crowned with Ra's Face, the Solar Disk
Thou! Thy blazing crown empowered with the Emerald Uraeus
Thou! the Heart of the World girt with a Serpent
Thou! the God enthroned upon Ra's seat lightening the girders of the Soul
Thou! Beyond Wisdom and Folly, Beyond male and female.
Thou! Seated on the Invisible Throne, Thy words illumine the worlds!
Thou! Master of Majesty and Might
Thou! Beautiful and Joyous
Thou! Clothed with Victory and Splendour
Thou! Standing upon the Firm Foundation
Thou! Lord of Initiation!—All Praise and Honor to Thee!
    For the Kingdom is Thine! Yea, the Kingdom is Thine!

*Getting it right, inside and out*
The invocation now, My Love, is complete, but there are certain finishing touches we need to do before we can apply our efforts to their fullest benefit. By now your visualization may be getting a bit fuzzy so we will sharpen it. This is called Vivid Appearance. We need also to remember that this visualization is the play of manifestation and points to something quite beyond itself. This is called the Recollection of Purity.

Thus, and often when you have developed sufficient skill quite quickly, the visualization is reviewed and refreshed. In the monasteries this is often done through a recitation of the description but it can be accomplished just by going over the details in your mind. Once this is firmly in mind, remember that each of the details of the description of the Deity-form and all of the attributes are symbolic presentations of the larger reality that is the path itself.

**Vivid Appearance—**
*Review in detail the visualization.* **Say:**
Ra-Hoor-Khuit has the head of a hawk and a human body with blue-black skin
He is crowned with the solar disk in which arises the emerald Uraeus
He wears the collar of the seven metals and twelve gems
He wears a white kilt, belted with gold, and his nemmes is sky-blue
He is seated on a 49-petaled red rose entwined with white jasmine
In his right hand is the Wast, the double scepter, while his left is empty

**Recollection of Purity—**
*Recollect that the emblems and ornaments are displays of His innate qualities.* **Say:**
His hawk head shows His consummate perspicacity
The solar disk, His compassionate, provident, and wrathful power
The emerald Uraeus, His relentless drive
His human body shows He has taken up the Middle Way
His blue-black skin shows His source in the Ground of Being,
The collar, His horizon being the Universe
The white kilt, His innate purity
The gold belt, the fullness of His capabilities
The sky-blue nemmes, His view as wide as the sky
The rose & jasmine, the female & male potentials that give rise to His being
The scepter is His rulership of form while
His empty hand shows His rulership of the formless

*Application: The Yogas of Recitation*
   Now that we have Ra-Hoor-Khuit present before us we generally want to achieve something. This can be simply advancing us along the path or removing the obstacles before us. As He is the embodiment of the Living Act of Accomplishing Will, you can say He is desirous of accomplishing your aims and the aims of all beings. As He is a wrathful destroyer of obstacles, His Energy is particularly good at removing them. In traditional forms this process can be quite elaborate. We, My Dear, shall begin with two simple modes: Arousing the Heart and Reciting the Mantra.

   Remember, My Love, that the Gods are impassive. However, while they do not share our emotions our passion for Them is a focus for Their power. We rely on Their compassion, but we have our part of the work to do and here we shape it through adoration. My heart tells me that we must ask as the Gods will not interfere unless we request Their aid. We behave as though we can say things to motivate the God, as though through flattery we will motivate action, but really we use it to arouse ourselves into receiving the blessing. It is therefore appropriate to use the Aka Dua chant which can be called the Mantra of Adoration:

**Arousing the Heart—**
**Sound or Sing, repeating:**
Aka dua / tuf ur biu / bia che fu / dudu nur af / an nuteru

As you repeat it see the Heart of Ra-Hoor-Khuit glow and radiate light. Do this at least one hundred times. It is worthwhile to use a mala or counting strand of 108 beads to do this. One mala's-worth is counted as one hundred and assumes you err on about eight of them. Once you are firm in seeing the Heart aglow or feeling His good wishes for you, you are ready to ask for benefit.

There are two major benefits to be requested. Blessings are the strengthening, enriching or improving any intention, situation or purpose. 'Removing obstacles' is the destruction of impediments to progress on the path.

**Requesting Blessings and Removing Obstacles—**
**Chant:**
Abrahadabra

*Repeat one hundred times and radiate Golden Wast Scepters throughout the Cosmos (see illustration). For Blessing, see the Head of the Wasts entering in enriching and empowering all beings. For Removing Obstacles, see the forked prongs at the lower end destroying obstructions to the accomplishment of the wills of all beings.*

For specific ends, besides radiating throughout the Cosmos, direct the focus of some of the Wasts to the representation your intent.

Do each of these recitations, including the Aka Dua, one hundred times. If you can't do them one hundred times, do them thirty-one times. If you can't do them thirty-one times do them eleven times. If you can't do them eleven times do them once each. But regardless, do them single-pointedly and with complete sincerity, remembering ever that these words are the embodiment of Ra-Hoor-Khuit in sound.

*Bidding the Deity Farewell*
So far our practice has been highly dualistic, reinforcing the distance between ourselves and the God. Before we can conclude we must destroy this useful but ultimately illusory viewpoint by uniting with Ra-Hoor-Khuit. In this practice we take three steps to accomplish this. We give thanks, we dissolve the Godform and then arise in the Body of Innate Union.

**Thanksgiving—**
*Having invited and welcomed the Honored Guest, address Ra-Hoor-Khuit from your heart and thank Him for His presence and many gifts, being as specific as you can.*

*Dissolving the Godform*
Having created this instance of the God by projecting from ourselves, in conclusion we gather that which we have projected back into ourselves.

## Radiating Out and Gathering In—
**Sound:**
AL— *and the universe dissolves into the Form of RHK, forming a golden sphere around the Deity and you.*
**Sound:**
AL— *and the Form of RHK dissolves into the golden sphere*
**Sound:**
AL— *and the golden sphere dissolves into your body. Rest and remain in the natural state of the mind as long as you can.*

**First,** sound the Deity's seed syllable, AL, and radiate golden honeyed light in all directions dissolving the Universe into a golden sphere which surrounds both the Deity and your body.

**Next,** sound the syllable again and, this time, the Deity's form and your own dissolves inseparably into the Golden Sphere, obliterating all vision except of golden light.

**Finally,** sound the syllable one last time, and dissolve the sphere slowly into your own body which scintillates with gold; Ra-Hoor-Khuit, like water being poured into water, becomes 'of one taste' with you.

At some point while you are resting you will either fall back into discursive thought and concepts will begin proliferating in your mind, or the impelling force of your Bodhicitta-compassion will drive you from the womb of the Void like a fish leaping from water. It is time to arise in that form of Ra-Hoor-Khuit that looks exactly like you, for you are none other than Ra-Hoor-Khuit incarnate as yourself. This is the Body of Innate Union.

## Arising in the body of Innate Union—
*Arise again in our own forms, inseparable from RHK and the Ground, the Union of Appearance and Openness,* **Saying:**
There is success. I am the Hawk-Headed Lord of Silence & of Strength; my nemmes shrouds the night-blue sky. Hail! ye twin warriors about the pillars of the world! for your time is nigh at hand. I am the Lord of the Double Wand of Power; the wand of the Force of Coph Nia— but my left hand is empty, for I have crushed an Universe; & nought remains...The ending of the words is the Word Abrahadabra... AUM Ha!
*Sounding "AUM Ha!" release all attachment and rest in an uncontrived state of mind.*

*Post-Transformational Practices*

Dear One, after every practice we distribute the merit of our work for the reasons we discussed before. But when doing a more elaborate practice like this invocation of Ra-Hoor-Khuit, two more intentions are best brought into play as a way of stepping down from the forces we have been working with and placing ourselves in the right attitude to go out into the world. The first reminds us of the nature of the work we have just done and is called Behavior after Transformation. The second is a salute to and blessing of the path on which we journey and is called the Earnest Wish. After these we dedicate the merit as usual and conclude the practice session.

This next verse is spoken after all of the work is done as a reminder of the attitude to take once the practice session is over. It serves as a concluding statement of intent to keep the mind and feelings in the right place once the work is done. It also recalls for us the playful nature of this spiritual work which greatly supports our success and points to the great secret that empowers it: all phenomena within and without the practice are created by the same means. Yes, My Love, you are making your reality, so please do a good job.

**Behavior after Transformation—**
**Say:**
All form, energy, and thought show forth primal, bornless presence.
May this play of manifestation develop my body, speech, and mind.
Through this practice may I attain complete realization
and lead all living beings to also attain.

At (nearly) the end of our practice it is also a good time to wish well for your tradition and mode of practice. Blessing is a most powerful way of wielding good, and at this point in your process you are in a very good position to perform a blessing. The following Thelemic Blessing has the dual advantage of blessing the Way and all Beings and so is another act of compassion.

**Earnest Wish—**
**Say:**
May the Law of the Aeon, beyond which there is none,
As open as the Star-lit heaven, the Thelemic Way,
Guide all to the accomplishment of their True Wills, the Great Work,
The Summum Bonum, True Wisdom and Perfect Happiness.

Finally, for all of the reasons we discussed above, we dedicate the merit of our practice. Here is the dedication verse:

**Dedication of Merit—**
Say:
May the benefit of this act and all acts
Be dedicated unto the Complete Liberation and Supreme Enlightenment
Of all beings, everywhere, pervading space and time, so mote it be!
May the benefits of practice, mine and others'
Come to fruition, ultimately and immediately
And I remain in the State of Presence. —A *(sound Ah)*

# 8

# Arising As

My Darling, all that has gone before is just the appetizer. While powerful in itself for magical purposes, and one other we will come to later, the function of your practice at first was to build your relationship to the Deity. Only when we know the God well enough can we call Him, and only when we have grasped His essence can we *be* Him. Through our power of transformation that comes from understanding the Void-nature of Being, we become and so manifest the Gods and Their blessings in the World. This way of invoking is called 'Arising As' and is where you will spend most of your time and effort. It is so called because having dissolved the world into the Void-Ground, you then recreate it with yourself arising from the ground as the Deity.

Once you have established a good connection with Ra-Hoor-Khuit through worship and the practice of Generation in Front, through study and the contemplation of His nature, you may be ready to invoke Him through 'Arising As.' You are fortunate to have a teacher to introduce you to the God and instruct you in the details of practice, and your teacher can help you know if you are ready to practice this advanced form. But those who are on their own will need to rely on the God to give them a sign in dream or waking life that the connection has been established. This is one very important reason why fervor and sincerity in Generation in Front is necessary. While dispassionate themselves, the Gods respond to passion.

The differences between Arising As and Generation in Front are few but crucial. Since I know that by this point you have practiced with diligence and intensity, fully memorizing the practice of Generation in Front, I will discuss the changes necessary to that rite to make it useful for Arising As in summary.

The full version of the ritual is as usual available for download from the website. It is good to have it alongside you while reading this chapter.

The opening of the ritual is for the most part the same as before, but you can drop out the Dedication Vow and the Invoking Lineage verses if you desire. The substantive changes begin once you are Dissolved in Shunyata. To Arise As sound and see Ra-Hoor-Khuit's seed syllable 'AL' as before but do so centered on where your body would have been if it existed. Use the same approach to generate the body of the godform, but instead of doing this in front of you, do it *as* you. When you say the Salute, "Ra-Hoor-Khuit hath taken his seat," etc., hear it as though it is said to you. This typifies most of the following actions.

When you Adorn the body with Syllables it is your new body that has the form of Ra-Hoor-Khuit that wears the syllables. Feel your divine body, speech, and mind scintillate with power as they arise.

Then it is the time to Call the Knowledge Being. Here is an odd moment of duality when your personality, My Love, makes another brief appearance, but if you have learned the lessons of the Body of Innate Union, this will not be too confusing. You are temporarily using the polar power of duality to draw the Spirit of the God to you. Instead of happening in front of you, when you get to the verse, "Appear on the throne of Ra..." the Khu leaves the lintel of the Gate and stoops through the top of your head into the hollow shell that was your body but which now you are maintaining by visualization in the form of the Deity, and alights on the AL at your navel. He expands to fill you with each line of the verse uniting with and empowering each of the dimensions of your being. Your Heart-Mind is filled with the Divine Presence with 'Khu.' Your Energy-Speech is filled with the Divine Presence with 'Ka.' Your Body is filled with the Divine Presence with 'Khabs.' And at last you are suffused with bliss with 'Aum.'

Once stable, Seal in the Spirit with your incantation of Abrahadabra. Let each letter of the Word of Manifestation arise and light up each Sephira in your Divine Body as you say it, one letter per sphere including Daath, descending both with and as the Lightning Flash. The Word Itself, shouted, spoken or whispered, has the character of the roar of thunder.

Next, perform the Initiation by the Solar Gods, conjuring Them, then visualizing and feeling that They are pouring the nectar on 'your' head, then dissolving into you. This time you hear Them speak to you.

**Initiation by the Solar Gods (Arising As)—**
**Say:**
From the Abodes of Life, I conjure the Sun!
**Sound:**
A— (Ah) *Call for aid from all Realized Beings, the Ground of Being Itself and the Potential for Enlightenment in all Beings. These arrive in the form of the Solar Gods: Khephra, the Beetle in the East; Ra, the Hawk-headed Man in the South; Atum the Man in the West; Het-Hoor, the Woman with Cow-horns and Solar*

*Disk in the North; Heru-ra-ha in the form of the Winged Disk in the Center (above). They each bear a crystal flask filled with glowing white nectar formed from innumerable white letter 'A's, and array Themselves about Ra-Hoor-Khuit.*

**Sound:**

A— *They pour their blessing nectar onto and through the top of His (Your) head and filling Him like a flask to overflowing. The overflow becomes the Solar Disk on His head with the Uraeus Serpent erect within it.*

**Sound:**

A— *The God now initiated, the Solar Gods dissolve and pour themselves into the God, becoming 'of one taste' with Him, and the image becomes alive and sparkling.*

**Say:**

Oh! thou art overcome: we are upon thee; our delight is all over thee: hail! hail: prophet of Nu! prophet of Had! prophet of Ra-Hoor-Khu! Now rejoice! now come in our splendour & rapture! Come in our passionate peace... Come! lift up thine heart & rejoice! We are one; we are none.

Now you are an instance of the God. Naturally the world notices and proceeds to offer the delights of the senses and praise. It is important that even as you say or sing the Offering verses and the Praise, you experience them being made to you. Traditionally, one visualizes male and female minor Deities appropriate to the offerings giving the offerings to you in the form of the Deity. We are fortunate to have the images on the Court Cards of the Tarot to work with. All sixteen can have their place but at least see the four princesses bringing you each of the four elements, and the others, emblems of offering. I commend to you the imagery from the Thoth deck, and their cards can be placed on or about the altar, if you have one set up, as representations. As the offerings are in essence the experience of the senses you can also simply focus on each of your senses and let what you are experiencing at that moment be the offering itself. There is a profound power in this, My Dear.

So far the change has been mostly one of perspective. Instead of having the action occur in front of you, it occurs here to you. But now comes the most important difference. After reinforcing the visualization (Vivid Appearance) you must firmly grasp the 'Ego of the Deity'. This is the part that gives this method of invocation its great power. Having built up the form of the Deity, you must now identify with Its identity. Think, as it were, "I am none other than Ra-Hoor-Khuit". Look out on the world in your mind through the character, wisdom and power of the God. Enjoy the sense pleasures as the God. Remember all of His relationships and deeds as your own. Merge your whole being as best as you can with Ra-Hoor-Khuit, whose form you wear and whose power you would wield. Success in this is the measure of the success of the invocation.

Once this is done, Recollect the Purity of the visualization and go on to perform the Yogas of Recitation. Watch the light radiate out from you, and take pleasure and satisfaction in the transformation you are working upon the world. If there is some specific magick you would do, this is where you would do it.

**The Yogas of Recitation—**
1. Realize the AL from which Ra-Hoor-Khuit was generated in His (Your) heart. Draw in a deep breath, sound **AL** and radiate golden, honeyed light over all beings (including Yourself) fulfilling the accomplishment of their wills. On the inhale gather up and gather in the wills of all beings setting the AL aglow. 100x
2. Chant **Abrahadabra** and radiate golden wast scepters throughout the Cosmos and see the forked prongs at the lower end destroying obstructions to the accomplishment of the wills of all beings. 100x

*Dissolving the Godform*
Rather than simply gathering up the Deity into ourselves to conclude, since we are Arising As, we go even deeper, joining with the Deity in the source from which He arose. This next part is much like Entering into the Ground and uses our accumulated wisdom and the Deity's seed-syllable to return all to the Void-nature of its being.

**Fulfillment without signs—**
**Sound:**
AL— *and the universe dissolves into the Form of RHK.*
**Sound:**
AL— *and the Form of RHK dissolves into the golden 'AL' at the heart.*
**Sound:**
AL— *and the 'AL' at the heart slowly, from the bottom feet up to the topmost point, dissolves into sheer Openness. Rest—*

**First,** sound the Deity's seed syllable, AL, and radiate golden honeyed light in all directions dissolving the Universe into your divine body.
**Next,** sound the syllable again and, this time, dissolve the divine body into the seed syllable resting at the heart.
**Finally,** sound the syllable one last time, and dissolve the syllable into space, slowly from bottom to top and go off into Shunyata with it. Rest and remain in the natural state of the mind as long as you can.

But this time, as you Arise in the Body of Innate Union, realize that the Success of which you speak is your inseparable Union with the God.

Finally, conclude as before.

# 9

# Fulfillment

Darling One, in this type of practice there are three major phases, empowerment, development and fulfillment. Empowerment or introduction into the space of the ritual, also called initiation, is a process similar to but different and more elaborate than the one used in the ritual and will be addressed in the next section. Traditionally this is both the starting point and a necessary prelude to any ritual of this type. This writing assumes the reader has either been helped by the formal introduction the empowerment gives or is forgoing that resource. You know of course, My Love, how that applies to you. When you perform the empowerment activity in the rite, you are recapitulating the formal empowerment, however you came by it, reinforcing its blessing.

Naturally, even with empowerment the process of acquiring the power and benefit of this ritual is not instantaneous. It requires a significant investment of time and practice to gain its full measure and this phase of practice is termed 'Development.' It also is the name of the portion of the ritual from after the Dissolution into the Ground up to and including to the Yogas of Recitation. What follows after is the 'Fulfillment' portion of the rite and is even more suitable for magickal application. It will take some work to get there. Traditionally that would require further repetition and contemplation of the mantra in its simplest form, and more elaborately can include practices with chakras and nadis, winds and drops, sephiroth and paths, as the various traditions term them.

In the Tibetan context, the teacher would say that one must repeat the mantra of the God one hundred thousand times per syllable of the mantra before going on to full application of the Fulfillment phase. So for the mantra of Chenrezig, "Om Mani Peme Hung", one would have recited it six hundred thousand times.

If you are not working with a teacher you will have to judge for yourself when it is time to work this phase in full, as we discuss below, but in the meantime some Fulfillment-level practice is done in Development-level work just in a very simple form. When you deepened your practice with the Arising-As mode, you were taught to re-enter Shunyata as the Deity and re-emerge in the Body of Innate Union, using the verses of Success (AL3.69-75). This is what we must now elaborate on.

The Fulfillment phase comes long after the ritual is learned by heart. In it the ritual itself may be done quite rapidly or in an abbreviated manner. The ritual itself may be reduced to simply sounding the seed syllable of the Deity, or even less. By this point your skills must have developed such that you can maintain the visualization and grasp the divine ego without wavering.

Fulfillment can also be practiced in two modes, with and without signs. 'With signs' is the method of maintaining the godform while performing inner yogas, concentrating and moving energy throughout the body along with certain visualizations. These are essentially the kriya and kundalini yogas. Learn these from masters of those arts or on your own, My Dear, but for the most part they lie beyond the scope of this work. When mixed with Deity Yoga such as this, and Bodhicitta, they form a powerful means towards enlightenment: the practice of the Tantrayana.

What makes this phase truly different is that once you have fully grasped the godform you can then continue the practice all of the time while combining it with the inner yogas. From here will all the truly profound benefits arise. The prime exemplars of success in this are the 84 Mahasiddhas venerated by both Hindus and Buddhists. They were ordinary people from all walks of life who received practices from their teachers and applied them diligently. Many of them raised the understandable objection that they had families to support and so had no time for practice. They were taught after they had mastered the Development phase how to blend the practice with their livelihood so that one reinforced the other and true enlightenment dawned. I highly recommend the study of their stories to you.

'Fulfillment without signs' is the simpler of the two. This is the form presented in the 'Arising As' version of the ritual, and labeled as such. The task is to return the Deity and the godform you wear to the Ground out of which it arises and there collect more power, wisdom and compassion. Then, like a fish leaping from the water, as it is traditionally described, you re-arise from the Ground as the Deity fully exercising its powers. The essence of this is the union of appearance (the godform) and emptiness (the Ground), so that you become fully an expression of the power, wisdom, and compassion, the living providence of the Ground of Being.

The method is similar to the Entering into Shunyata, except it is the Deity doing the process and the Deity who arises from the Void at its end. First, having fully put on the godform, sound the seed syllable of the Deity and with it dissolve the Universe into your divine body. Next, sound again, and dissolve the divine body into the seed syllable resting at the heart. Then, sound one last time and slowly dissolve the syllable into space. Rest there in the natural state of the mind as long as you can. Eventually the force of your Bodhicitta will drive you from union with the Void, and into action in the form of the Deity you have invoked. Wield the mantra and the attributes of the Deity for the benefit of beings. This is such a good place to start that even in the Development phase we do some of this.

My Love, even while I am 'open-sourcing' such a profound practice as I have so far written you, there are lines which even I will not cross. There are many highly specialized, subtle and profound practices of inner yoga that without proper coaching can be worth-
less, or worse, harmful. Wisdom coun-
sels me not to put them into print.
The more general practices are safe, and              Had, brow,
wholly helpful and healthy, and only strengthened    white
by the Divine form you wear. Since they are so
common I will only discuss them in summary. If       Re, throat,
you desire more, find a qualified teacher. At least  red
now you know what to look for.

When you have decided it is time to practice
the Fulfillment with Signs take on the Godform       Nu, heart,
of Ra-Hoor-Khuit and focus on the inner world        blue
of your Divine Body. Choose either the view of
the Chakras or the Sephiroth, in other words the
Yogic approach or the Qabalistic.                    AL, navel,

If you use the Chakras, you have two other           gold
choices to make. You can apply the traditional visualizations of the Chakras and their seed syllables
(Sanskrit or Tibetan) or you can work with the Egyp-  Sma, loins,
tian ones presented here. The other choice is how     red & green
many Chakras to use. We start off with four in the
Empowerment and in the Adornment with Sylla-
bles. Five, seven, nine, and far more than that can   Ta, base,
be visualized. There are marvelous and easy to find   black
teachers and written works available that can do a far better job in instructing you in these practices. The only difference is that you first put on the God-form and then do the yoga.

We are not entirely reliant on Eastern methodologies. Our tradition has long used the Qabalah, which ultimately derives from Mesopotamia, for the structure of our divine cosmology, our anagogic path, and for our subtle an-thropology. It is an application of this last that assists us here. The Tree of Life can be considered a map of the human esoteric nervous system. As with the yogic work, I will leave you to the published and extant teachings for the basics but for our purposes there are a few points worth making.

Like with the Chakras, one decision to be made is how many. Remember that you can use the whole Tree, or just the Middle Pillar. The commonly taught method has the specific advantage of drawing power downward and generative or moving into manifestation, and thus is useful for magick. This is nicely balanced by the common approach to the Chakras, which is upward and anagogic.

The Hermetic Qabalah of the Magi provides you with Tarot Trump imagery which is of potent application when cycling energy between the Sephiroth on the paths between them, supporting the Hebrew Letters and their sounds. Exploring this while reinforced with divine presence is exhilarating. Also, the Hermetic Qabalah makes less use of Yahweh, Who has objections to other Gods.

While the foregoing are of known and particular use, I would be remiss, My Love, if I did not mention that the Taoists, the Druids, the Norse and many others have similar 'yogas' that may with great effect be applied here. I will leave such exploration in your most capable hands. Just remember to have care, and seek harmony, intensity, and compassion in all of your practices.

# 10

# Initiation

Beloved, You and some others had the chance to learn this rite from one who knows it, even one who composed it. Many reading this work will have to take the long road of approach through Generation in Front. At some point, having done the necessary development, you and they may find it desirous to introduce new practitioners to the rite. There is a distinct method to this that should be applied to produce the best foundation for those who would walk this way.

The best way to start with a ritual of this type is to be initiated into it. This may not be available to the first person creating such a ritual but they will have the advantage of either the long work of developing the rite, extensive practice of the rite or, if very fortunate, the direct deity inspiration that leads them to create the rite. I will provide the structure and keys for success, you will need to create the rite as it is best to practice it for yourself and your students. But do not do this at all until you are ready. At a distance from a teacher, you must rely on the Deity to know when that time is.

To compose the initiation, collect resources associated with Ra-Hoor-Khuit. Invocations, songs, emblems and images are all useful. There are many available in the Book of the Law, the other Thelemic Holy Books (especially Liber Tzaddi) and in works of classical Egyptian culture. Nor should you neglect contemporary transformations of traditional symbols. Your creativity will guide you. The initiation can be made more or less complex in a wide variety of ways. Including drama, physical activities, food or music, for example, can make the rite more impactful.

The purpose of the rite is to tincture the being of the aspirant with the various parts of the Deity's nature. In the Buddhist mode these are called 'kaya' or bodies and so a Deity or 'Wisdom Being' is said to have several 'bodies'. The short list is an emanation body (Nirmana-kaya), the physical one; a Treasure-house body (Sambhoga-kaya), a sort of astral body that displays the symbolic form of the Deity; and a Truth body (Dharma-kaya), the essential or noetic body. In Qabalistic terms the first corresponds to the Assiac body, the second to a combination of the Yetziratic and Briatic levels, and the last to the Atziluthic world. Some schools add to this a number of specialized 'bodies' that enlightened beings sometimes manifest. For our example we will use the short list and add to it the 'Body of Perfection', which is the union of the three mentioned.

Structurally there are two main portions of the ritual: before the aspirants join the initiator and afterwards. During the 'before' part, you as the initiator prepare yourself and the ritual materials for the initiation. When the aspirants join you, you will then convey to them the initiation.

*Preparing the Implements*

**First,** perform the rite as above and arise in the form of Ra-Hoor-Khuit. Complete everything through the Fulfillment phase, including any energy work you wish to do. There is nothing wrong with reciting the final verses of well-wishing and the distribution of merit, although they can be omitted at this point, but regardless of where you stop, do not drop the godform, and maintain yourself firmly in the ego of the Deity. It will be as Ra-Hoor-Khuit that you will perform the initiation.

**Next,** as the Deity, dissolve all of the ritual implements and the ritual space itself into Shunyata and then reconstitute them back from the Void. This is the purification.

You may well evolve your own way of doing this, but you have already been introduced to the following:

**Purifying the Implements—**
*Point to the objects with finger, wand or vajra and* **Say:**
So with thy all; thou hast no right but to do thy will.
Do that, and no other shall say nay.
For pure will, unassuaged of purpose,
delivered from the lust of result, is every way perfect.
The Perfect and the Perfect are one Perfect and not two; nay, are none!
*If you can manage it, with the final word spoken, 'none', dissolve all into the void.*
*If not, follow the verse with the Egyptian seed syllable for the void, 'nun'.*
**Sound:**
Nun— *and all dissolves. Repeat as many times as required.*
*Now, to reconstitute the tools and space* **Sound:**
Abrahadabra!— *and all reappears as pure manifestations of the Ground of Being,*
*suitable for use in a Divine Initiation.*

You can also name each of the items in turn as you pull them from the Void, or you can sound relevant seed syllables. Thus 'Vajra' and generate the Dorje, 'Ram' or 'Ray' and generate the fire, or 'Zain' and draw forth a sword.

At this point you still hold the form and the mind of Ra-Hoor-Khuit, yet the tools you are about to use, while pure, are 'blank.' You will now give them their character by transforming them into the Deity, or better said, an instance of the Deity. Yes, you are Ra-Hoor-Khuit and the tools will also be Ra-Hoor-Khuit, and, eventually, the aspirants will be Ra-Hoor-Khuit. This is part of what it means to be a God, that You are a general principal of Being, instantiated throughout all of Being. Here, You create an instance of Yourself (as Ra-Hoor-Khuit) with the outer form of ritual tools so that you can use them to communicate your Spirit to the aspirants. Who else could do as good a job of this as Yourself?

**Transforming the Implements—**
*Perform the rite again in the In Front manner. You can go back to the very beginning, but you can also just start from the Dissolution into the Ground. Dissolve and recreate the previously purified objects in the same manner as you purified them, but this time draw them forth with the seed syllable of the God.*
**Sound:**
AL— *then proceed through the rite as you did when generating in front, but never losing sight of the fact that you are also the God.*

When it comes time for the yogas of recitation, run the mantras of Ra-Hoor-Khuit as many times as you can. One thousand times for each 'body' is a good beginning, using a different mantra for each. The approach we are using applies three objects: a vase, an image, and a symbol, one for each of the three bodies and about which we will say more shortly. Each mantra has as its focus one of these objects.

To transfer the mantra to the object make a cord of red, black, and white threads, for the three schools of Power, Wisdom and Compassion, and braid them together. Attach one end to the vase, drape the length about the image and the symbol and hold the other end at your heart. As your recite the mantra see its letters and syllables travel from your heart to the objects and dissolve inseparably into them.

**Empowering the Implements—**
*Empower the Vase with the Word of Manifestation,* **Repeating:**
ABRAHADABRA
*Empower the Image with the Mantra of Adoration,* **Repeating:**
Aka dua / tuf ur biu / bia che fu / dudu nur af / an nuteru
*Empower the Symbol with the Syllables of Empowerment,* **Repeating:**
Had-Re-Nu-AL

*Enter the Aspirants*

Now you are ready for the aspirants to enter, but they need to be prepared. It is best to have someone else do this so you can concentrate on your work and on maintaining the godform. They need to be given the following instructions, a handout for which can be found on the website.

They must understand that this introduction is an initiation in which their effort is at least as important as that of the initiator. Without their effort, alignment to purpose, and ready karma, this will only be a series of vain activities.

They are to take a vow to dedicate the benefit of their practice to all beings. Besides having them say this vow in the ritual, it may be worthwhile, and proper disclosure, to have them sign a sheet with the text of the vow. This also help you record who has received the introduction. Other personal data like contact information can be beneficially collected at this time.

When they enter the ritual space they are to visualize you, My Dear, as Ra-Hoor-Khuit, hawk-headed, blue-black skinned, with a sky-blue nemmes, a wast or dorje in your right hand, and the left, empty. You are to be seen seated on a throne with a rose seat, jasmine armrests and winged disk as the backrest. On your head is a red solar disk with an emerald Uraeus serpent arisen in it. A white winged-globe is at your brow, a red solar disk at your throat, a blue nu-pot at your heart and a golden AL-syllable at your navel. They are also to see all of the tools as actually being another instance of Ra-Hoor-Khuit on the altar.

Have them visualize themselves also as Ra-Hoor-Khuit but only as hawk-headed, with blue-black skin, sky-blue nemmes and with wast or dorje. But no solar disk, no syllables, these will come later.

If they have one, you may also wish the aspirants to place their malas (strands of beads for counting mantra) on the altar when they enter, along with any offerings and other objects to be blessed by the rite. Roses and flowers, food and drink, statuary and other precious and talismanic items are common.

They should also be told a summary of the major action during the introduction, namely that everyone is to chant the mantra (provided on a handout, and available on the website) while one at a time each approaches the altar for the blessings, and that this will happen three times. After these three are done, the introductor will hold aloft a crystal, representing the non-dual nature of the introduction and deity-yoga to formulate the Body of Perfection. They are to gaze at the crystal and sound 'A' with the introductor and then let their minds settle into their natural, uncontrived state until your signal.

Tell them that after the introduction the practice itself will be first presented as a guided meditation. Then it will be taught in detail and there will be time for any questions. Be sure to have breaks planned between each phase. This is very intense concentration and you do not wish to tire or strain the aspirants.

When you are ready and they have been duly informed, have the aspirants enter and lead them through the preparatory phases of the rite: Refuge and Bodhicitta. Do this by reciting the prefatory verse and then having them respond along with you with the activity words. They should have a handout to refer to (see website).

**Refuge—**
**Initiator Says:**
Nu is my refuge as Hadit my light;
and Ra-Hoor-Khu is the strength, force, vigour, of my arms.
**All Sound:**
'Ah' — 'Ah' — 'Ah'
*If they are not familiar you will need to instruct them in the method of Refuge in this manner. For this reason, and due to the attention demand of this rite, it is often worthwhile to teach the preliminary practices of Refuge, Bodhicitta, Empowerment, the Four Immeasurables, Dissolution into the Ground and the Distribution of Merit at a separate teaching session before the initiation itself.*

**Generating Bodhicitta—**
**Initiator Says:**
Remember all ye that existence is pure joy;
that all the sorrows are but as shadows;
they pass & are done; but there is that which remains.
**All Say five times:**
All is pure and present,
And has always been so.
To this realization
I commit myself—
    Pure and Total presence.

All together repeat the Dedication Vow dedicating their practice and invoke the aid of those who have gone before with the Lineage prayer.

**Dedication Vow—**
**All Say:**
I hereby dedicate my practice
of this Invocation of Ra-Hoor-Khuit
to the benefit of all beings, including myself,
and upon attaining to the realization that it gives,
I dedicate that power to aid all beings
to the supreme realization called Enlightenment.

**Invoking Lineage—**
**All Say:**
I invoke those who have gone before me
I invoke the Shamans, the Magi and the Witches who founded my practices
I invoke the Orders that preserved and transmitted the Way
I invoke the Teachers who taught me the Way
Bless me, sustain me, empower me in my practice
For I am one of you, true heir and descendent
In me the Way lives, aid me!

Invocations, prayers and offerings are next to set the mood and to ask for blessings for the aspirants. This puts the aspirants into a receptive state. While the 'bodies' are being introduced the aspirants can chant, make music or otherwise be kept occupied and in focus. Begin with reciting Liber Tzaddi together, having again provided a handout. Add to this by your right ingenuity.

When all is in readiness the aspirants must indicate and affirm that it is their will to take initiation. To do this they make a formal request.

**Request for Instruction—**
**Aspirants Say:**
Beholding the Teacher before us as Ra-Hoor-Khuit,
Lord of the Aeon, Lord of Initiation,
resplendent with all good qualities and intentions,
We request introduction into the space of this ritual
that we may perform the invocation of Ra-Hoor-Khuit
and attain quickly to the God's High State.
This is our will, pure, unassuaged of purpose,
and delivered from the lust of result.
Please grant us instruction!

Acknowledge their request and, after you recite the opening verse for each body, have them begin with the chant and any other supporting activities like music. Drums, thunderous horns and cymbals can be very effective here.

**Nirmana-kaya Empowerment—**
**Initiator Says:**
Abrogate are all rituals, all ordeals, all words and signs. Ra-Hoor-Khuit hath taken his seat in the East at the Equinox of the Gods; ...Hoor in his secret name and splendour is the Lord initiating.
**Aspirants Repeat while each comes in turn for Empowerment:**
Abrahadabra

As Abrahadabra is recited in unison again and again, one at a time each aspirant comes before you. They should place themselves in a yin or receptive state, but if they must kneel for you to reach them, assure them that they do not kneel to you, Dear One, but to the God.

The first body to be introduced is the Nirmana-kaya, the physical body. The method is to take the vase, which is a vessel of liquid, and touch the vessel to the body, speech, mind and will centers of the aspirant (brow, throat, heart, and navel), and then pour a bit of liquid into their hands which are held with the right in the palm of the left, face up as a cup. They drink the liquid and wipe the remnants on their crown. The liquid is traditionally a saffron infusion, which is a lovely golden yellow color attributed to enrichment and growth, and tastes pleasant. Soaking a few strands of saffron in water overnight makes this. Any vessel will do but the Tibetans have a small vase called a bhumpa that is perfectly suited. It has a wide belly to hold plenty of liquid, a narrow spout to control the pour and a deep lip at the top by which you can gracefully hold the vase for pouring. Since this part is about the 'physical' body we use a physical substance that is taken from the outside and brought inside the aspirant by them drinking it. Upon blessing the syllables of empowerment arise on the bodies of the aspirants: the white winged globe on the brow, a red solar disk on the throat, a blue nu-pot at the heart, and a golden AL at the navel.

When all have been served move on to the next body and say the opening verse, the Adoration of Ankh-af-na-khonsu. Being lengthy there is no profit in presenting it here again, but note you can use the original from Liber AL or the modified form as shown before (p. 60) if you please.

## Sambhoga-kaya Empowerment—
**Initiator Says or Sings:**
*the Adoration of Ankh-af-na-khonsu*
**Aspirants Repeat while each comes in turn for Empowerment:**
Aka dua / tuf ur biu / bia che fu / dudu nur af / an nuteru

This body is the Sambhoga-kaya, the treasure-house or energy or astral body. This is the body that the Deity presences to you in visions. So, to effect the introduction, use an image of Ra-Hoor-Khuit as its embodiment, such as the Aeon Trump of the Thoth Deck, or a small statue may suffice. Touch the image to the brow, throat, heart and navel of the aspirants when they come before you. Upon blessing, the full godform, just as you wear, appears on the aspirants. When this part is complete, move on to the next body by reciting the verse.

The third body is the Dharma-kaya, the essence, truth, or law body. Use some abstract object for this. A dorje or phurba are traditional and as Ra-Hoor-Khuit is the Lord of the Double Wand of Power, such will serve. The Dorje or Vajra, which is the Thunderbolt of Zeus and thus the Lightning Flash of Abrahadabra, is convenient and effective. Weapons, stones, objects of nature or art can be used to represent the mind-essence of the Deity. Since these objects are consecrated in the first part of the rite there is a lot of room to be creative here. Here you will have an extra task to complete the blessing. When you touch the aspirants' chakras with the (assuming) dorje, touch it first canted forty-five degrees from vertical to one side and touch again similarly canted to the other side forming an 'X' shape, alluding to the Sign of Nox, to seal in the blessing while saying the secret fourfold word, 'Do what thou wilt.' When the blessing is complete the ego of Ra-Hoor-Khuit spontaneously arises in the aspirant's minds.

**Dharma-kaya Empowerment—**
**Initiator Says:**
Oh! thou art overcome: we are upon thee; our delight is all over thee: hail! hail: prophet of Nu! prophet of Had! prophet of Ra-Hoor-Khu! Now rejoice! now come in our splendour & rapture! Come in our passionate peace... Come! lift up thine heart & rejoice. We are one; we are none.
**Aspirants Repeat while each comes in turn for Empowerment:**
Had-Re-Nu-AL
**Initiator Says:**

| Do | *touch brow* |
|------|----------------|
| what | *touch throat* |
| thou | *touch heart* |
| wilt | *touch navel* |

Finally, when all have been blessed, we move beyond the dualism we have upheld for the sake of delivering the rite. The last part is the 'Body of Perfection'. This is the union of the three kayas and shifts the attention of the aspirants away from the initiator. For this hold up a clear crystal and sound a grand 'Ah.' Have everyone, including yourself, focus their attention on the crystal with the sounding and then remain in the natural state of the mind afterwards for as long as possible. In this, body, speech, and mind unite in action, joined to the Ground, the inherent perfection from which all arises and places all present, aspirant and introductor alike, on the same level.

**Body of Perfection Empowerment—**
*Hold a crystal aloft and* **All Sound:**
Ah *and all focus with uncontrived mind on the crystal. Rest—*

Wrap up with the concluding activities and then teach the invocation itself. This can easily take about four hours not including ramp-up.

# *Beyond Here, Dragons*

The remaining chapters detail practices that can only be considered in *beta*, that is, they are insufficiently tested, in marked contrast to the foregoing rites. As they are more social in nature, or dealing with wider issues, they are presented here for the benefit of the student. Use with care.

# 11

# Yab-Yum

My Dear Love, the art of magick is a progressive science, taught only on the basis of "I told you that story to tell you this one." All the foregoing was to bring us here, but it was necessary for you to master each and all of it before the doors before you now can open.

The work must be memorized because you will not have text available to you. You must be able to move with the drama and to move the drama through the skill of your practice, otherwise it will be just playacting. To the extent that you have achieved mastery so far only will the gates of this rite open to you.

For this, Beloved, is the practice of Union, where a couple join in the forms of the Gods to find divine rapture and exultation. Some say that only through the physical practice of union with a suitable partner can the supreme enlightenment be achieved. All I know is that this is the most demanding form of practice and carries with it the great peril of reversing all your good work through attachment and obsession. Yet, it is only through risk that we can scale the greatest heights.

This form of the rite is especially suited for a heterosexual couple, although other forms of union are neither excluded nor disparaged. However, male homosexual practice may find more traction in the Union of Horus and Set, and it is reported that a practice of female Union is to be found in Liber Stellæ Rubeæ, but those lie beyond this simple work.

Here, we use the power of Love and Desire, focused by Will, to recreate the world and ourselves into a realm of divine play. Perhaps, My Love, it would be better to say that we are then able to see the world as it is and has always been.

Both partners should be skilled in the practice. This is a meeting of equals, yet it is a practice of the Left Hand, in which the female is especially exalted. Behaviors of the Left Hand are an especially Hindu path, suited to a culture of profound inequality in which under normal conditions the woman is quite subservient to the man. In Tantric spirituality this imbalance is redressed. Miranda Shaw's *Passionate Enlightenment* is a good source for understanding this tradition. It is customary in that society for the woman to sit on the left-hand of the man and serve his food with her right. Tantra sees in the Woman the embodiment of the Divine Feminine, the Source of all Life and Being and so the situation reverses itself. The man should seat himself to the left of the woman, and she controls the engagement. He is to serve her with his left hand and defer to her in every way. She is the Source of all Power, the Granter of Boons, the Embodiment of the Goddess and to be worshiped. In due time this is reciprocated, but only after proper reverence has been made.

External conditions are not very important when we practice alone. Our eyes are mostly closed and we need only to be undistracted. When we work with another our outer senses are used more and so our physical space must be well prepared. Besides remaining undisturbed, beauty and comfort are necessary requirements. Your desire, resources, and capabilities will determine how elaborate are your preparations.

Once prepared, She and He meet at an auspicious time. Ra-Hoor-Khut and Ra-Hoor-Khuit are Solar Divinities and so this rite is well aspected at the stronger times of the day: dawn, noon, and sun-set, but the midnight hour also has its charms.

They may well first sit side by side and perform the practice, arising as the Gods, or They may do so before entering the space. Or, if sufficiently skilled, they may proceed directly with the rite modified as described below. The full text will be found on the website.

**Refuge—**
As ever, They begin with refuge, but here They take special refuge in the Consort. In the basic practice of refuge the Buddhist takes refuge in the Buddha, the Dharma and the Sangha. The Tantric Buddhist takes refuge in the Guru or Teacher as the embodiment of the Buddha, the Deva or Godform as the embodiment of the Law, and the Dakini/Daka, the female and male consort, respectively, as the embodiment of the Community of Fellow Practitioners.

In the case of our rite, They say together the verse, then as They sound the first 'A' (Ah) They specifically include the Consort as one of the Beings to whom They pray for Refuge, or even as the Sole Source of Refuge, the union of all others. With the second 'A' They see the Light of Blessing specifically come from the Consort to empower Themselves. With the third 'A,' as ever, They flood the world with Good.

### Generating Bodhicitta—

Next, when They generate Bodhicitta, They address the Verse to each other as an admonition and take the Vow of Purity together, each a witness for the Other.

### Empowerment—

Up until this point, They have behaved as equals. Now this ends and the Behaviors of the Left Hand begin. She takes Empowerment directly from Nuit, quickly as per the rite, or more elaborately as presented in the chapter on the Dissolution into the Ground, or by such other means as She may discover. Regardless of means She will, thus empowered, take on the form of Ra-Hoor-Khut before Him and adorn herself with the Syllables. It is to Her, the Daughter of Nuit, that He shall go for empowerment.

He shall pray the verse, "Who am I and what shall be the sign?"

And She will respond, "So she answered him, bending down, a lambent flame of blue, all touching, all penetrant, her lovely hands upon the black earth, & her lithe body arched for love, and her soft feet not hurting the little flowers: Thou knowest! And the sign shall be my ecstasy, the consciousness of the continuity of existence, the omnipresence of my body."

He shall perform the gestures of taking up the Syllables and She shall support this with such actions as she is inspired. In the end, they sound the grand 'A' together and contemplate Their nature being of one taste.

### The Four Immeasurables—

She begins by declaring the Verse as He listens to its admonition. They have practiced, we assume, the basic Four Immeasurables in the preliminaries. If not, they may do so here. The basics cultivated, They perform the Special Four Immeasurables suited to lovers, as follows.

They sound 'A' to give voice and power to Their actions as oft as is needed, but if needed other words may be said. He performs this as worship, She receives it as Her due. He pours out His Loving-Kindness, accompanied by gestures and caresses. She reciprocates in due form. This inspires His Compassion, which He offers in an earnest embrace. She reciprocates in due form. He is moved by this to give Her pleasure and take Joy therein. She reciprocates in due form. And in this midst of this delight, His Body, Speech and Mind remain in Equipoise, and She joins Him therein. This is none other than love play, by which all do the Four Immeasurables, spontaneously but unknowing. The Consorts do this at will, yet here it is only the prelude.

### Entering the Ground—

When the Consorts have gathered up Their power in Their play, They unite Their bliss with emptiness by saying the verse to affirm Their will, and as needed the syllables, and remain as long as possible in the Void-Nun.

Arising—
*When They can no longer bear it,* **He prays,**
O Nuit, continuous one of Heaven, let it be ever thus;
that men speak not of Thee as One but as None;
and let them speak not of thee at all,
since thou art continuous!
**She whispers:**
None, breathed the light, faint & faery, of the stars, and two.
For I am divided for love's sake, for the chance of union.
This is the creation of the world,
that the pain of division is as nothing,
and the joy of dissolution all.
**Together They sound 'AL.'**
*In the Void arises the Golden Syllable AL.*
**Together They sound 'AL.'**
*The Golden Syllable shines light throughout the Void filling All Space.*
**Together They sound 'AL.'**
*The Light returns with the collected Will of All and forms a Golden Sphere around the Golden Syllable.*
**Together They sound 'AL.'**
*The light streams out dissolving the Golden Sphere, draining it like a lake which reveals Ra-Hoor-Khut & Ra-Hoor-Khuit in Union enthroned on a Rose.*

**Sealing with Syllables—**
**She says:**
Burn upon their brows, o splendrous serpent!
**He says:**
O azure-lidded woman, bend upon them!
**Together They sound:**
HAD—RE—NU—AL *and a white winged globe appears on the brow of each of the Gods, a red solar disk appears at Their throats, a blue Nu pot appears at Their hearts, and a gold AL appears at Their navels.*
**Together They sound from the small 'A' in the heart of the Nu pot:**
A— *(Ah) All unite in bliss and the Gates of the Duat open above Them, the Hawk perching upon the threshold.*

**Calling the Knowledge Being—**
*They say or sing the Adoration and the Hawk stoops into each of Their bodies to take up His place.*
**Together They sound:**
Abrahadabra (3x) *reviewing the Sephiroth, the planets and the elements and sealing in the Knowledge Being.*

**Initiation by the Solar Tathagatas—**
*Next they call for initiation by the Solar Gods with the conjuration.*
**Together They Say:**
From the Abodes of Life, I conjure the Sun!
**Together They sound: 'A'**
*And the Solar Gods Arrive.*
**Together They sound: 'A'**
*The Gods pour their blessing nectar onto and through the top of the Couple's heads.*
*The overflow becomes the Solar Disks.*
**Together They sound: 'A'**
*The Solar Gods dissolve and pour themselves into the Divine Consorts, becoming 'of*
*one taste' with Them.*
**Together They say:**
Oh! thou art overcome: we are upon thee; our delight is all over thee: hail!
hail: prophet of Nu! prophet of Had! prophet of Ra-Hoor-Khu! Now rejoice!
now come in our splendour & rapture! Come in our passionate peace...
Come! lift up thine heart & rejoice! We are one; we are none.

**Offerings—**
*He now makes such physical and spiritual offerings to Her as They have prepared,*
*one at a time and slowly that She may enjoy them. When satisfied,*
**She says:**
May blessing now be poured To the Hawk-headed mystical Lord!
*Then She likewise makes offerings to him.*

**Praise—**
*Praise can be offered one to the other, or spoken together, but at this point in the rite*
*the Consorts may well be in such state as to make all praise spontaneous and accom-*
*panied by their play.*

*The Inner Work*
   In the midst of Their play the Consorts continually review Their Vivid
Appearance, reinforce Their Firmness of Ego and Recollect the Purity of the
symbolism.

**Arousing the Heart and the Yogas of Recitation—**
*Likewise, They arouse the heart of the Other with the Aka Dua chant and then per-*
*form the yogas of recitation, sounding AL and Abrahadabra.*

**Fulfillment without and with Signs—**
*In due time, the Consorts dissolve the Godforms, and the whole Universe, only to*
*spring forth back into being in Their play, and practice such Yogas with Signs as*
*They are skilled. Indeed, My Love, this may in fact be the longest part of Their play,*
*for here, in union, practicing the Yogas with Signs, gains Them the most benefit for*
*Their Liberation and Enlightenment, and such Magick as They would work.*

Thus it is right, meet, and proper before They conclude to recite the verses of Success for Arising in the Body of Innate Union, knowing Their own forms to be not other than that of the Gods They have invoked, the Union of Appearance and Openness.

At long last They earnestly recite the Behavior after Transformation and the Earnest Wish and, finally, Dedicate the Merit.

# 12

# A Thelemic
# Ganachakra
### a 'mass' performed
### in the tantric manner

Now, Dear One, our work takes a deeper turn. It will require your mastery of the foregoing and real creativity to apply what follows. Be sure you are ready; forget not to ask the God.

All of the practices above must be fully internalized before you can enter the Ganachakra, the circle of gathering. It is composed in two parts, Source and Armature. The Source is the essential rule that tells what must be done. The Armature is a kind of explanation which includes examples of how some parts may be done.

This is a rite to be performed by a circle of initiates of the Thelemic Way. It was specifically written for those who have accomplished the rite I have been teaching you but by applying other views within the spectrum of Thelema, there are many other ways of working it. This is why the Source is so sparse and open to interpretation, and why the Armature is so limited. As the risk and benefit increases with adding a partner, it does so exponentially when done as a group. Be wise, be wary, test your companions with subtlety. Every choice matters.

# Source
Abrahadabra!
Taking the view every way perfect,
Making no difference between any one thing and any other thing,
The Scarlet Woman and the Beast establish an altar
To the 3 of the chapters, to the 1 face the magi wear,
To the many protectors of the Law, to they of the 6 destinies,
and to the 8 obstructing classes

**The Higher**
With Abrahadabra
Offerings of the 5 nectars are effectuated
And offered to the 5 types of invited guests

**The Inner**
AL!
With Abrahadabra
Each Scarlet Woman in the Circle becomes Ra-Hoor-Khut

With Abrahadabra
Each Beast in the Circle becomes Ra-Hoor-Khuit

With Abrahadabra
He offers Her, in turn or at once, the 5 nectars
And adores Her with the Song Aka Dua

With Abrahadabra
She offers Him, in turn or at once, the 5 nectars
And adores Him with the Song Aka Dua
AL!

**The After**
With Abrahadabra
They remain in union, in contemplation,
Each Beast adores Ra-Hoor-Khut with Song while
Each Scarlet Woman adores Ra-Hoor-Khuit with Song
Until the grand Aum is sounded and with Ha!
All is shattered into Not

After an aeon and an aeon and an aeon
The leftovers are gathered on cracked plates,
The dregs are dribbled on the scraps,
Charged with "So with thy all. . ."
Until "nay, are none!" and
Effectuated with Abrahadabra,
Unto the low ones these offerings are given

Then gathering up, declaring wishes and wills,
Dedicate the benefit to all and for the success of practice,
and radiate all with A—

*Let this Mass, this Thelemic offering circle,*
*Be a benefit to all and to all who gather to practice it*
*May it be sealed with that Bornless Spirit*
*That is about it like a Thunderbolt, and a Pylon, and a Snake, and a Phallus,*
*And is in the midst thereof like*
*the Woman that jetteth out the milk of the stars from her paps*
*Abrahadabra!*

# Armature

This is a rite in the spirit of a 'mass', a group eucharistic ritual written in the Thelemic tradition performed in the tantric manner. 'Tantric' in this case means in the manner of the offering pujas as used in both the Shakti and Buddhist traditions. There, the practitioners would gather to form the mandala of the deities they will be invoking. Arrayed in couples each would, after the invocations, treat their partner as the embodiment of the deity. They would offer and receive offerings maintaining the view of their partner and all present as deities, the place as a divine mansion, and the offerings as 'nectar and ambrosia' and yet, in the non-dual manner, all 'of the same taste'. In this kind of rite the offerings may be symbolic or as actual as means and courage allow.

While this rite was composed with a certain invocation of Ra-Hoor-Khuit in mind, any suitable invocation will serve. Per the language of Liber AL vel Legis, of the officiants and the practitioners, He is called the Beast and She is called the Scarlet Woman, yet "Deem not too eagerly to catch the promises; fear not to undergo the curses."

Begin by opening the space: banish and consecrate at will, or simply take Refuge and generate Bodhicitta. Perform such preliminary invocations and accumulations as seem fit, such as the Mahayogatantra Invocation of Ra-Hoor-Khuit.

Next, invoke the presence of the guests into the space or upon the altar. There are 5 kinds of guests in this rite: The three deities of the 3 chapters of the Liber AL are the embodiment of the three gems, the basis of refuge and empowerment. Ra-Hoor-Khuit and Ra-Hoor-Khut are the specific deity-forms of the rite expressed dyadically. This Deity's essential form, beyond the duality of gender, is Ra-Hoor-Khu and so the 'one face.' All of the protector spirits and deities who have vowed to protect the Law receive their place of honor. All of the beings of each of the six different ways of incarnating, namely Deity, Asura/Titan/Jealous God, Human, Animal, Hungry Ghost, and Hell-Being, are each made offering to. Lastly the beings of the eight obstructing classes, those that interfere with our work, are fed as well. In a non-dual practice such as this we invite everyone, friend and foe to the table. Thus we practice viewing all 'with the same taste'.

The principal officiants can be in the center of the space, with all arrayed about them, or to one side, perhaps the East. They can be the physical objects of worship or they may set up a physical altar. The congregation is best arrayed in pairs but solitary practice is possible with sufficient visualization.

What follows are examples of one way the offerings might be done:

**To the Three of the Chapters**
Had!–Ra!–Nu!– Abrahadabra!
Nuit! Hadit! Ra-Hoor-Khuit
To you and all your host we offer,
Form, Sound, Smell, Taste, and Touch,
The Whole of Space,
Father's Milk and Mother's Blood, and the Fruit of Existence
Come and Enjoy!

**To the One Face the magi wear**
Had!–Ra!–Nu!– Abrahadabra!
Ra-Hoor-Khu
To you and all your host we offer,
Form, Sound, Smell, Taste, and Touch,
The Whole of Space,
Father's Milk and Mother's Blood, and the Fruit of Existence
Come and Enjoy!

**To the Protectors:**
Had!–Ra!–Nu!– Abrahadabra!
Hermes, Hekate, Ishtar, Inanna, Tahuti, Maat, Therion, Babalon
To you and all your host we offer,
Form, Sound, Smell, Taste, and Touch,
The Whole of Space,
Father's Milk and Mother's Blood, and the Fruit of Existence
Come and Enjoy!

**To the Six Destinies**
Had!–Ra!–Nu!– Abrahadabra!
To all ye Deities, and Jealous Gods,
To ye Humans and ye Animals,
To ye Hungry Ghosts and Hell-Beings,
To you and all your hosts we offer,
Form, Sound, Smell, Taste, and Touch,
The Whole of Space,
Father's Milk and Mother's Blood, and the Fruit of Existence
Come and Enjoy!

**To the Eight Obstructing Classes**
Had!–Ra!–Nu!– Abrahadabra!
To all ye Deities,
To ye Furies and ye Fates
To ye Daemons and Caco-Daemons
To ye Fairies and Elves
To ye Nymphs and Dryads
To all ye Elementals, Salamanders, Undines, Sylphs and Gnomes
To ye Trolls and Dwarves
And to ye Dragonkind
To you and all your host we offer,
Form, Sound, Smell, Taste, and Touch,
The Whole of Space,
Father's Milk and Mother's Blood, and the Fruit of Existence
Come and Enjoy!

The offerings themselves are traditionally a set of foods and behaviors forbidden by Brahmanic culture or Buddhist monastic rule. Human flesh, cow, horse, dog and elephant meat were all on the menu. Other forms used feces, urine, pus, semen and menstrual blood. This was accompanied by liquor and/or other intoxicants and sexual union, both because of their forbidden nature and for the stimulation they provide the rite. In general these substances were replaced by the visualization of them along with the physical use of meat, fish, grain, liquor or wine, and sex. The five-foldedness refers to the five senses and so the offerings are referred to under that rubric in classical rites and our current example. To this is added "space" as a euphemism for Mind (Nous or Rig-pa), the male and female basis for existence, and an emblem of the enjoyment of existence as a whole.

Practically, set up your offerings using such food as you have. If the group is small enough, plates are set up for each person or couple. If the group is larger, the plates are passed among the congregation. To practice 'all same taste' one takes from every plate or cup that passes regardless of personal inclination toward the contents. Using the 5-senses method, an item for each of the senses can be offered: a rose, a candle flame, chocolate, a bell, and a caress are all examples.

To begin the inner offerings, the principal officiants, and all others to the extent that they are able, invoke and take on the godform of Ra-Hoor-Khuit or Ra-Hoor-Khut as appropriate. Once the godforms are present each partner makes offering to each other holding the view of the other as the Deity. AL2.34-44 make good verses with which to open the inner offerings. There is no speech during the inner offerings except the Song. Rather, each offering is made, one at a time, in silence or while singing. This serves as a prelude to physical or symbolic union. Remain in union practicing the view as long as the view can be maintained. When difference is again made between one thing and other thing it is time to conclude the inner rite and proceed to the after. Negotiate this with silent signals.

To make offerings to the low ones, the guests too weak or corrupted by their karmic condition to enjoy the higher offerings, take the scraps of the offerings, put them on the worst plate available, preferably one with cracks. Then sprinkle the dregs of the wine or other drink on it. This is to permit the lower guests to enjoy the benefits of the rite converted down to their level where the offerings will not be poison to them.

All of the offerings are effectuated with 'Abrahadabra'. This is done by pointing at the arrayed offerings with wand or hand or aught else and sounding the Word. In the specific case of the after offerings, or any where else desired, the offerings are charged with verses 42-45 of AL1, starting "So with...".

In conclusion, offer prayers, wishes and wills for the future, and dedicate the benefit of your work to all beings. This will preserve and project your work wide in the world.

*Mangalam! May this knowledge go aright!*

# 13
# A Thelemic Phowa

*Homage to the bornless awakened nature in all beings.*

Dearest, it is suitable that at the end of the work we come to a practice for the end of life. But it comes too late. I have great comfort in knowing you are in a far better place, but your death is an unimaginable loss. For nearly two years cancer slowly destroyed your brain and assailed your mind with torment. I began this work before those days, in the spring of renewed love. There was and is no one else I could have written this precious work to, for you were my partner in so much; I held you dear in this too. You, who wrote so easily, helped my faltering and inky speech more than any human and all I produce henceforth will be blessed by your kind tutelage.

No less is the calm of my heart and mind, as you brought to so many by your profession. When I was in the depths of blackest depression you set me to task to write the practice that follows. Its impact on me was immense but dwarfed by the rite you and our family of choice created for me to end my perennial spiral into death and come renewed into life. Because of you I live without that crushing weight of melancholy, never to return.

I feared for you, but in the end, your Goddess and the Lamas delivered you, and you had no need for this practice or this little work. Your journey, blessed in the end with a sigh and a smile, I know took you to where you could rest and heal and be a Goddess yourself as ever you were.

Smile, my Beloved, on all the good you did, on the innumerable beings you benefited, and let all the rest just wash away. For this is life, that we may do the best we can. That is the only perfection we can have. As at the beginning, so here at the end, in memoriam, I dedicate this Work to you.

Death comes in many guises. Sometimes it comes as the recognition that who one is must die. The wise one knows of two choices, physical extermination or the death that is called initiation. In the mid-1990s, I found myself in such a situation and so I called upon my magickal family to aid me. The rite itself was a profound success, clearing much that was dead or suffering from my soul, and this success was rooted in the preparations they had asked me to make.

One of the preliminary meditations I was told to do was a Pagan, properly Thelemic, variant on the Tibetan practice called Phowa, the transference of consciousness. This is a meditation that permits one to leave the body through the crown of the head upon death and enter directly into the state of enlightenment or into the Pure Land of (usually) the Buddha Amitabha, where one would then have the opportunity to practice under perfect conditions and attain to complete enlightenment. This is a very deep and profound practice, no less so for the setting as for the consequences: one practices this at the point of death. Success secures liberation or at least good rebirth. If done wrong or wrongly understood, it becomes a source of distraction at a time when we most need our wits about us.

My family had little idea what they asked of me when they told me to compose a Phowa. It is a powerful practice that if properly done will actually cause a softening on the top of the head or even an opening to emerge there which the consciousness will use to exit upon death. If practiced too strongly before the proper hour of death, it can actually cause the death of the practitioner. Nonetheless a very simple practice arose that was used to great effect. The reader should again be warned. I am no Lama, or Tulku; I have no right to dispense such a practice, yet there is need, so I do this. If you truly desire to enter the path of Phowa practice seek out a qualified teacher or at least read about it in *The Tibetan Book of Living and Dying* by Sogyal Rinpoche.

*Place yourself in a comfortable position, spine straight, best if it is vertical.*
*Take Refuge, Generate Bodhicitta.*

*Recite these verses to establish focus and attitude:*
1. I am the Heart; and the Snake is entwined
2. About the invisible core of the mind.
3. Rise, O my snake! it is now the hour
4. Of the hooded and holy ineffable flower.
5. Rise, O my snake, into brilliance of bloom
6. On the corpse of Osiris afloat in the tomb!
7. O heart of my mother, my sister, mine own,
8. Thou art given to Nile, to the terror Typhon!
9. Ah me! but the glory of ravening storm
10. Enswathes thee and wraps thee in frenzy of form,
11. Be still O my soul! that the spell may dissolve
12. As the wands are upraised, and the aeons revolve.

13. Behold! in my beauty how joyous Thou art,
14. O Snake that caresses the crown of mine heart!
15. Behold! we are one and the tempest of years
16. Goes down to the dusk and the Beetle appears.
17. O Beetle! the drone of Thy dolorous note
18. Be ever the trance of this tremulous throat!
19. I await the awaking! The summons on high
20. From the Lord Adonai, from the Lord Adonai!

At the base of the spine sound       Had—
At the Heart sound                   Re—
At the Crown of the head sound       Nu—
(Note the different arrangement of syllables from the forgoing practices.)

Cycle this over and over driving your attention and consciousness up to the top of
your head along with the syllables, and as the pressure begins to mount stay with it
as long as you can. When it becomes too much release the energy out the top of your
head with a long 'Ah'. If you were dying you would sound the cutting syllable, 'Phat!'
(pronounced 'pet!'), which would cut you free of your body. The verses and the sounding can be repeated as many times as the practitioner wishes in a sitting.

At the end Distribute the Merit.

These lines are the first verse of Aleister Crowley's The Book of The Heart
Girt with a Serpent. To help in the understanding of the power of the verses
used above, the following analysis is offered. This does not exhaust the meaning of the words, but rather gives a preliminary indication of their import:

1-2     The heart here is the heart of one's being, that which gives us our
sense of selfhood and individuality, the core of one's consciousness or
mind. The snake is the Kundalini serpent whose power, in rising up, will
thrust the consciousness of the practitioner out of the body at death.

3       The serpent is enjoined to rise up, it is now time.
4       This flower is a phallic emblem of the fruition of the lifetime about
to end and the entering into the state of enlightenment upon death.

5-6     Again the serpent is enjoined to rise up to its full stature likened to
a blossom in full bloom. Meanwhile, the body of the practitioner is looked
upon as the corpse of Osiris which is both the seed from which the illumi-
nated being shall arise and the fertilizer for the process.

7-10    Now the heart of the practitioner is viewed dualistically as other, and
this other is the very Goddess to whom the practitioner aspires. The reason
for the necessity for illumination is given; that this heart is under the do-

minion of maelstrom of the worlds of form. The heart of the practitioner, while also being not other than inherently the very goal of the practitioner's aspiration, is so blinded by frenzy that the heart does not know itself to be that goal.

11-12  Then the work begins. Stillness is required of the heart and soul in order to liberate the practitioner. Only in the still clarity of mind can this spell be worked to dissolve the imprisoning walls of form. The powers, the wands, which invoke and direct this liberation are raised up into action while all the time in the world necessary to complete the process is invoked into presence.

13-14  The process has begun and quickened into bliss as the serpent force rises to and above the heart (both as heart chakra and as mind).

15-16  The practitioner declares the unity of self and the process, identifying with the serpent, rising beyond time which fades into night. The serpent becomes pure becoming, symbolized by the Khephra Beetle. The word 'Kheper' in ancient Egyptian means to become, to transform, or to be born. Its canonical form is actually a view of the top of the human skull showing the cranial sutures and the fontanel gap through which the practitioner is going to exit the body. The Khephra Beetle taking wing was a symbol to the Egyptians of the soul taking flight from the chrysalis of the body.

17-18  The drone is the sound of the Beetle taking flight and the mantra the practitioner will be saying. This verse includes the aspiration vow to keep the mantra going until success has been attained.

19-20  Now the practitioner places herself in the state of yearning and awaiting necessary to the success of the practice. Adonai here is the innate, already enlightened and liberated aspect of the practitioner that will raise her up and guide her to the true nature of existence, presented here as the Goddess who is mother, sister, and lover to the practitioner.

*May this knowledge go aright.*

# Mahayogatantra Invocation of Ra-Hoor-Khuit
### In Front, Level 1

**Refuge—**
**Say:**
Nu is my refuge as Hadit my light;
and Ra-Hoor-Khu is the strength, force, vigour, of my arms.
**Sound:**
A—     *The unveiling of the company of heaven*
A—     *I am uplifted in thine heart;*
               *and the kisses of the stars rain hard upon thy body.*
A—     *This shall regenerate the world, the little world my sister,*
               *my heart & my tongue, unto whom I send this kiss.*

**Generating Bodhicitta—**
**Say:**
Remember all ye that existence is pure joy;
that all the sorrows are but as shadows;
they pass & are done; but there is that which remains.
**Say:**
All is pure and present, and has always been so.
To this realization I commit myself:
Pure and Total presence.

**Dedication Vow—**
**Say:**
I hereby dedicate my practice
of this Invocation of Ra-Hoor-Khuit
to the benefit of all beings, including myself,
and upon attaining to the realization that it gives,
I dedicate that power to aid all beings
to the supreme realization called Enlightenment.

**Invoking Lineage—**
**Say:**
I invoke those who have gone before me
I invoke the Shamans, the Magi and the Witches
Who founded my practices
I invoke the Orders that preserved and transmitted the Way
I invoke the Teachers who taught me the Way
Bless me, sustain me, empower me in my practice
For I am one of you, true heir and descendent
In me the Way lives, aid me!

**Empowerment by Ra-Hoor-Khut—**

| Say: | See: |
|------|------|
| Had! | *Sound,* |
| The manifestation | *and a golden Winged Globe* |
| of Nuit. | *appears before you* |
| | |
| Nu! | *Sound, and the Globe folds its wings* |
| the hiding of Hadit. | *and is wrapped in darkness like the night sky, hidden* |
| | |
| Abrahadabra; | *Sound, and the darkness is riven by lightning* |
| the reward of | *The Lightning Flash forms into Ra-Hoor-Khut,* |
| Ra Hoor Khut. | *with flesh of lapis lazuli, hair of jet,* |
| | *red Egyptian garb with gold ornaments.* |

**Adorning with Syllables—**
Sound:

HAD—  *On the Brow of Ra-Hoor-Khut appears a White Winged Globe*
RE—  *At the Throat of Ra-Hoor-Khut appears a Red Solar Disk*
NU—  *At the Heart of Ra-Hoor-Khut appears a Blue Nu Pot*
AL—  *At the Navel of Ra-Hoor-Khut appears a Golden Aleph-Lamed*

**Receiving Empowerment—**
Say:

Who am I and what shall be the sign? So she answered him, bending down, a lambent flame of blue, all touching, all penetrant, her lovely hands upon the black earth, & her lithe body arched for love, and her soft feet not hurting the little flowers: Thou knowest! And the sign shall be my ecstasy, the consciousness of the continuity of existence, the omnipresence of my body [the unfragmentary non-atomic fact of my universality].
Sound:

HAD—  *Reach out to the White Winged Globe on the Brow of Ra-Hoor-Khut with both of your hands. Lift it off Her brow (where it yet remains) and draw it to your own, trailing light back to Hers. Place it on your brow and feel the purification of your flesh pour throughout your body.*

RE—  *Reach out to the Red Solar Disk at the Throat of Ra-Hoor-Khut and draw it to your throat, whereupon appears a Red Solar Disk empowering your speech and energy.*

NU—  *And again with the Blue Nu Pot at the Heart of Ra-Hoor-Khut, to your heart whereon appears a Blue Nu Pot empowering your mind.*

AL—  *Finally from the Golden AL at the Navel of Ra-Hoor-Khut draw to your navel, whereon appears a Golden AL empowering your will.*

A—  *(Ah) Sound, and Ra-Hoor-Khut and all realized beings sound with you. Ra-Hoor-Khut dissolves from back to front until only the syllables remain which then travel up the beams of light and unite with the syllables on you, granting all empowerments and becoming of one taste with you. Rest.*

The Four Immeasurables—
**Say:**
Compassion is the vice of kings: stamp down the wretched & the weak: this is the law of the strong: this is our law and the joy of the world. (AL2.21)
**Sound (4, 16, or 20x):**
A— *(Ah) Awaken Loving Kindness–Compassion–Joy in their Joy–Equanimity toward*
*Yourself–All who are close to you–All who are connected to you–*
*All who you know of–To the non-objectified All*

**Entering the Ground of Being—**
**Say:**
So with thy all; thou hast no right but to do thy will.
Do that, and no other shall say nay.
For pure will, unassuaged of purpose,
delivered from the lust of result, is every way perfect.
The Perfect and the Perfect are one Perfect and not two;
nay, are none!
**Sound:**
Nun— *and you take on the godform of Nun or Nuit, i.e., anthropomorphic with a nu-pot (see Syllables of Adornment) on your head, while you observe the universe of Form dissolving into the Formless Ocean of Nun.*
**Sound:**
Nun— *and your body dissolves slowly from below into the Formless Ocean, leaving only the spherical nu-pot.*
**Sound:**
Nun— *and the nu-pot slowly dissolves from the bottom, through its girth, to its mouth which dissolves off into the Void-Ocean of the Nun like the sound of a singing bowl. Rest—*

**Conjuring the Godform—**
**Perceiving silently:**
Then the priest answered & said unto the Queen of Space, kissing her
lovely brows, and the dew of her light bathing his whole body in a sweet-
smelling perfume of sweat:
   *Out of the heartache of separating from the Whole of Being pray fervently as did*
   *the Scribe—*
**Say:**
O Nuit, continuous one of Heaven, let it be ever thus;
that men speak not of Thee as One but as None;
and let them speak not of thee at all,
since thou art continuous!
   *Then imagine your whisper as her voice in response. . .*
**Say (whisper):**
None, breathed the light, faint & faery, of the stars, and two.
For I am divided for love's sake, for the chance of union.
This is the creation of the world, that the pain of division is as nothing, and
the joy of dissolution all. *This Light and collected Will forms a Golden Sphere*
*around the Golden Syllable.*
**Sound:**
AL— *the syllable AL arises alone in and from the Void, self-luminous and metallic*
   *Gold and hangs in space before you.*
AL— *golden, honeyed light radiates from the syllable throughout all Space and re-*
   *turns on the inhale gathering up the power of Ra-Hoor-Khuit into the syllable*
   *transforming it into a Golden Sphere or Egg.*
AL— *the light goes out from the syllable blessing all beings throughout space, fulfill-*
   *ing their wills and dissolving the Golden Sphere, draining it from the top down*
   *like a lake leaving in its midst the form of Ra-Hoor-Khuit enthroned on a Rose.*

**Saluting the God—**
**Say:**
Ra-Hoor-Khuit hath taken his seat in the East at the Equinox of the Gods...
Hoor in his secret name and splendour is the Lord initiating.

**Adorning with Syllables—**
**Say:**
Burn upon their brows, o splendrous serpent!
O azure-lidded woman, bend upon them!
**Sound (all in one breath):**
HAD—RE—NU—AL *and a white winged globe appears on the brow of Ra-Hoor-*
*Khuit, a red solar disk appears at His throat, a blue Nu pot appears at His heart,*
*with an "A' inside it, and a gold AL appears at His navel.*
**With the next breath sound:**
A— *(Ah) from the small 'A' in the Nu pot, and all is suffused with bliss, and the*
*Gate of the Duat opens before you.*

**Calling the Knowledge Being (Khu)**
**Say or Sing:**
I am a Lord of Earth, and I
    The inspired forth-speaker of Heru;
For me unveils the veiléd sky,
    The self-made _use own name_
Whose words are truth. I invoke, I greet
    Thy presence, O Ra-Hoor-Khuit!

Unity uttermost showed!
    I adore the might of Thy breath,
Supreme and terrible God,
    Who makest the gods and death
To tremble before Thee:—
    I, I adore thee!

Appear on the throne of Ra!
    Open the ways of the Khu!
Lighten the ways of the Ka!
    The ways of the Khabs run through
To stir me or still me!
    Aum! let it fill me!

The light is mine; its rays consume
    Me: I have made a secret door
Into the house of Ra and Tum,
    Of Khephra and of Ahathoor.
I am Mage, O Heru,
    The prophet _use own name_!

By Therion my breast I beat;
    By Babalon I weave my spell.
Show thy star-splendour, O Nuit!
    Bid me within thine House to dwell,
O wingéd snake of light, Hadit!
    Abide with me, Ra-Hoor-Khuit!

**Sealing in the Spirit—**
**Sound:**
Abrahadabra! (3x)

**Initiation by the Solar Gods—**
**Say:**
From the Abodes of Life, I conjure the Sun!
**Sound:**
A— *Call for aid from all Realized Beings, the Ground of Being Itself and the Potential for Enlightenment in all Beings. These arrive in the form of the Solar Gods: Khephra, the Beetle in the East; Ra, the Hawk-headed Man in the South; Atum the Man in the West; Het-Hoor, the Woman with Cow-horns and Solar Disk in the North; Heru-ra-ha in the form of the Winged Disk in the Center (above). They each bear a crystal flask filled with glowing white nectar formed from innumerable white letter 'A's, and array Themselves about Ra-Hoor-Khuit.*
**Sound:**
A— *They pour their blessing nectar onto and through the top of His head, filling Him like a flask to overflowing. The overflow becomes the Solar Disk on His head with the Uraeus Serpent erect within it.*
**Sound:**
A— *The God now initiated, the Solar Gods dissolve and pour themselves into the God, becoming 'of one taste' with Him and the image of which becomes alive and sparkling.*

**Greetings—**
*Welcome Ra-Hoor-Khuit in whatever manner seems best to you.*

**Offerings—**
**Say:**
May blessing now be poured To the Hawk-headed mystical Lord!
**Say or Sing:**
Had!—Re!—Nu!— Abrahadabra!
Ra-Hoor-Khu-it: To you and all your host we offer,
Form, Sound, Smell, Taste, and Touch, The Whole of Space,
Father's Milk and Mother's Blood, [and] the Fruit of Existence
Come and Enjoy!

**Praise—**
*Ouarda's verses may be used here, or Webster's short form below, or ad lib.* **Say:**
Thou! The Hawk-headed Lord of Silence and of Strength,
    Thy nemmes shrouds the night blue sky
Thou! Crowned with Ra's Face, the Solar Disk
Thou! Thy blazing crown empowered with the Emerald Uraeus
Thou! The Heart of the World girt with a Serpent
Thou! The God enthroned upon Ra's seat lightening the girders of the Soul
Thou! Beyond Wisdom and Folly, beyond male and female.
Thou! Seated on the Invisible Throne, Thy words illumine the worlds!
Thou! Master of Majesty and Might
Thou! Beautiful and Joyous

Thou! Clothed with Victory and Splendour
Thou! Standing upon the Firm Foundation
Thou! Lord of Initiation! — All Praise and Honor to Thee!
For the Kingdom is Thine! Yea, the Kingdom is Thine!

**Vivid Appearance—**
*Review in detail the visualization.* **Say:**
Ra-Hoor-Khuit has the head of a hawk and a human body with blue-black skin
He is crowned with the solar disk in which arises the emerald Uraeus
He wears the collar of the seven metals and twelve gems
He wears a white kilt, belted with gold, and his nemmes is sky-blue
He is seated on a 49-petaled red rose entwined with white jasmine
In his right hand is the Wast, the double scepter, while his left is empty

**Recollection of Purity—**
*Recollect that the emblems and ornaments are displays of His innate qualities.* **Say:**
His hawk head shows His consummate perspicacity
The solar disk, His compassionate, provident, and wrathful power
The emerald Uraeus, His relentless drive
His human body shows He has taken up the Middle Way
His blue-black skin shows His source in the Ground of Being,
The collar, His horizon being the Universe
The white kilt, His innate purity,
The gold belt, the fullness of His capabilities
The sky-blue nemmes, His view as wide as the sky
The rose & jasmine, the female & male potentials that give rise to His being
The scepter is His rulership of form while
His empty hand shows His rulership of the formless

**Arousing the Heart—**
**Sound or Sing, repeating:**
Aka dua / tuf ur biu / bia che fu / dudu nur af / an nuteru

**Requesting Blessings and Removing Obstacles—**
**Chant:**
Abrahadabra
*Repeat one hundred times and radiate golden Wast Scepters throughout the Cosmos.*
*For blessing, see the heads of the Wasts entering in, enriching, and empowering all*
*beings. For removing obstacles, see the forked prongs at the lower end destroying ob-*
*structions to the accomplishment of the wills of all beings.*

**Thanksgiving—**
*Having invited and welcomed the Honored Guest, address Ra-Hoor-Khuit from your*
*heart and thank Him for His presence and many gifts, being as specific as you can.*

**Radiating Out and Gathering In—**
**Sound:**
AL— *and the universe dissolves into the Form of RHK, forming a golden Sphere around the Deity and you.*
**Sound:**
AL— *and the Form of RHK dissolves into the golden sphere.*
**Sound:**
AL— *and the golden sphere dissolves into your body. Rest and remain in the natural state of the mind as long as you can.*

**Arising in the body of Innate Union—**
*Arise again in our own forms, inseparable from RHK and the Ground, the Union of Appearance and Openness,* **Saying:**
There is success. I am the Hawk-Headed Lord of Silence & of Strength; my nemmes shrouds the night-blue sky. Hail! ye twin warriors about the pillars of the world! for your time is nigh at hand. I am the Lord of the Double Wand of Power; the wand of the Force of Coph Nia— but my left hand is empty, for I have crushed an Universe; & nought remains...The ending of the words is the Word Abrahadabra... AUM Ha!
*Sounding* "AUM Ha!" *release all attachment and rest in an uncontrived state of mind.*

**Behavior after Transformation—**
**Say:**
All form, energy, and thought show forth primal, bornless presence.
May this play of manifestation develop my body, speech, and mind.
Through this practice may I attain complete realization
and lead all living beings to also attain.

**Earnest Wish—**
**Say:**
May the Law of the Aeon, beyond which there is none,
As open as the Star-lit Heaven, the Thelemic Way,
Guide all to the accomplishment of their True Wills, the Great Work,
The Summum Bonum, True Wisdom and Perfect Happiness.

**Dedication of Merit—**
**Say:**
May the benefit of this act and all acts,
Be dedicated unto the Complete Liberation and Supreme Enlightenment
Of all beings, everywhere, pervading space and time, so mote it be!
May the benefits of practice, mine and others'
come to fruition, ultimately and immediately
And I remain in the State of Presence. —A (*sound Ah*)

# Selected Bibliography

Beyer, Stephan. *The Cult of Tara*. Berkeley: University of California Press, 1978.

Blofeld, John. *The Tantric Mysticism of Tibet*. Boston: Shambhala, 1987.

Conze, Edward. *Buddhism: Its Essence and Development*. New York: Harper & Row, 1975.

Copenhaver, Brian P., tr. *Hermetica*. Cambridge: Press Syndicate of the University of Cambridge, 1992.

Cozort, Daniel. *Highest Yoga Tantra*. Ithaca: Snow Lion, 1986.

Crowley, Aleister. *The Holy Books of Thelema*. York Beach, Maine: Samuel Weiser, Inc. 1983.

Dowman, Keith. *Masters of Mahamudra: Songs and Histories of the Eighty-four Buddhist Siddhas*. Albany, NY: State University of New York Press, 1986.

Godwin, Joscelyn. *The Theosophical Enlightenment*. Albany: State University of New York Press, 1994.

Greer, John Michael. *A World Full of Gods: An Inquiry into Polytheism*. Tucson: ADF Publishing, 2005.

Guenther, Herbert, tr. *The Creative Vision*. Novato, CA: Lotsawa, 1987.

Guenther, Herbert, tr. *The Matrix of Mystery*. Boulder: Shambhala, 1984.

Longchen Rabjam. *The Practice of Dzogchen*. Ithaca: Snow Lion, 1989.

McEvilley, Thomas. *The Shape of Ancient Thought: Comparative Studies in Greek and Indian Philosophies*. New York: Allworth Press, 2002.

McIntosh, Christopher. *Eliphas Lévi and the French Occult Revival*. London: Rider and Company, 1972.

Shaw, Miranda. *Passionate Enlightenment*. Princeton: Princeton University Press, 1994.

Sogyal Rinpoche. *The Tibetan Book of Living and Dying*. San Francisco: Harper San Francisco, 1992.

Tsong-ka-pa. *Deity Yoga*. Ithaca: Snow Lion, 1981.

York, Michael. *Pagan Theology: Paganism as a World Religion*. New York: New York University Press, 2003.

## About the Author

Sam Webster, M. Div., Mage, has taught magick publicly since 1984. He graduated from Starr King School for the Ministry at the Graduate Theological Union in Berkeley in 1993. He is an Adept of the Golden Dawn and a cofounder of the Chthonic-Ouranian Templar order, as well as an initiate of Wiccan, Buddhist, Hindu and Masonic traditions. His work has been published in a number of journals such as *Green Egg, Reclaiming Quarterly, Mezlim,* and *Gnosis.* He founded the Open Source Order of the Golden Dawn in 2001 (www.OSOGD.org), and serves the Pagan community principally as a priest of Hermes.

He can be contacted through the publisher: info@concrescent.net.

## About the Cover Artist

Kat Lunoe studied painting and drawing at the Bridgeview School of Fine Art in New York City, and at the Repin Academy of Arts in St. Petersburg, Russia. She has exhibited work in several group exhibitions in New York City, and also holds a degree in psychology from Queens College, City University of New York. She is now based in Berkeley, and is a member of the Open Source Order of the Golden Dawn.

She may be contacted at 93kats@gmail.com.

## About Concrescent Press

Concrescent Press is dedicated to publishing advanced magickal practice and Pagan scholarship. It takes advantage of the recent revolution in publishing technology and economics to bring forth works that, previously, might only have been circulated privately. Now, we are growing the future together.

## Colophon

This book is made of Goudy Old Style using Adobe InDesign, Illustrator and Photoshop. The body was set and illustrated by the author, with the exception of *Anubis Kneeling* from Dover Clipart.

### Visit our website at
### www.Concrescent.net
*for scripts, graphics and conversation*
on Tantric Thelema *and future works.*

Breinigsville, PA USA
20 April 2010
236534BV00001B/4/P

9 780984 372907